DICTIONARY OF

EARTH
MYSTERIES

DICTIONARY OF

EARTH MYSTERIES

Janet and Colin Bord

Thorsons

An Imprint of HarperCollins*Publishers*

Thorsons
An Imprint of HarperCollins*Publishers*
77–85 Fulham Palace Road
Hammersmith, London W6 8JB
1160 Battery Street
San Francisco, California 94111–1213

Published by Thorsons 1996

1   3   5   7   9   10   8   6   4   2

Janet and Colin Bord assert the moral right to
be identified as the authors of this work

A catalogue record for this book
is available from the British Library

ISBN 1 85538 496 5

Printed in Great Britain by
HarperCollinsManufacturing Glasgow

Contents

Introduction

Someone not familiar with the concept of 'earth mysteries' might pick up this book and ask: What is it all about? Geology? Astronomy? Gardening? 'Earth mysteries' is in fact a relatively recent concept, less than 30 years old, which developed in the 1960s in the wake of renewed interest in Alfred Watkins' ley theories. But it does not have a clear-cut definition, meaning different things to different people. Broadly it can perhaps best be defined as a study of the past, from the earliest communities in Britain to recent times, and the way in which people have interacted with the land on which they live. Of particular interest are the stone structures which early man has left behind: What were they intended for? Did those early inhabitants of Britain have knowledge that has since been lost? What were their preoccupations, and how much of their belief-system has come down to us in the form of folklore, legend and mythology? These questions have spawned theories and fantasies of great variety and imagination, but rarely with any solid evidence to support them. The truth is that we don't know a great deal about the way early man thought, and we have to base our deductions on the fragmentary remains that are left, since there are no written records until we reach Roman times around 2,000 years ago.

What we have attempted to do in this dictionary is to introduce as many subjects that fall under the 'earth mysteries' umbrella as we can. The very nature of a dictionary means that we cannot go into any one subject at great length, but anyone whose appetite has been whetted can find more meaty books listed in the Bibliography. Nor can this book be definitive, since each researcher has his or her own favourite areas of research, which he or she is bound to concentrate on. As will perhaps become clear when you dip into this book, our speciality tends to be folklore. But we have tried hard to remain unbiased in our coverage, and hope that this book provides a useful starting point for further reading and research. Within the dictionary entries, words in bold type indicate other entries under those headings.

Although the concept of 'earth mysteries' was born in Britain, it has in recent years become a worldwide field of interest. We have of necessity had to confine this book to British earth mysteries, simply because there would not be enough space to do justice to the earth mysteries of the whole world. Some details of the wider picture can be found in other books, particularly those written by Paul Devereux, which we strongly recommend.

We have ourselves been involved in earth mysteries for nearly 30 years, having come into it at the time when Paul Screeton was starting to edit *The Ley Hunter* magazine (1969 to 1976), and writing our first book on the subject, *Mysterious Britain*, in 1972. Several more titles have escaped since then (*see* Bibliography on page 125), and many changes have taken place in earth mysteries, so that the new generation of seekers will find themselves entering a different world from that which was being opened up by John Michell, Paul Screeton, Paul Devereux and other stalwarts in the late 1960s. It is still an exciting world, with much more to be discovered. If this book sets you on the path of discovery, our efforts will have been of some use.

Janet and Colin Bord
Clwyd, April 1995

A

Abbots Bromley Horn Dance

A traditional **custom** with its probable origins in pagan **fertility** rituals, the Horn Dance takes place annually in September in a Staffordshire village. Six of the participants wear antlers, and they and their companions (a male Maid Marion, a hobby-**horse**, a fool, two boys and a musician) perform ritual dances at locations in and around the village. The custom has clear links with the worship of **horned gods** in Celtic Britain, and Abbots Bromley is in the territory of the old Celtic tribe the Cornovii, the 'Horned Ones'.

Location: Abbots Bromley, Staffordshire; the Horn Dance is held on the first Monday after the first Sunday after 4 September. OS ref: SK 082245.

Alignments

See **Leys**

Arbor Low

This puzzling **prehistoric site** is described as a **henge**, being archaeologically similar to **Stonehenge** and **Avebury**, though not so visually impressive. Its stones lie flat, and may always have been like that, or perhaps only propped up, as no evidence of holes in which they may have stood has been found. There are over 50 large stones, set in a circular area bounded by a bank and ditch, and looking something like a huge clockface from above. Being of limestone, they are dazzlingly white: this area of Derbyshire is known as the White Peak. The henge has been dated to the late **Neolithic** or early **Bronze Age**: later, but still in the Bronze Age, a tumulus was built into the outer bank, and a burial mound around 5 metres (16 feet) high, known as Gib Hill, was constructed a short distance away. This is an enigmatic site, clearly once of great importance, but now all trace of its rituals and ceremonies is gone, and its meaning is lost for ever.

Location: 7 kilometres (4½ miles) SW of Bakewell, Derbyshire. OS ref: SK 160636.

Arthur, King

Supposedly a king of Britain who lived around AD 500, despite much research no one has been able to pin Arthur down for certain. If he existed, he was probably a chieftain or warrior rather than a true king. He is mentioned in several early writings, such as the 9th-century *History of the Britons* by the cleric Nennius, who lists 12 battles in which Arthur was the victor; and his story features largely in the *History of the Kings of Britain*, written in the 12th century by Geoffrey of Monmouth. But this account of the 5th and 6th centuries is unreliable, probably mixing fact with fantasy, and it is difficult to know where fact ends and fantasy begins. Geoffrey's account brought the magician **Merlin** into the story, and Arthur's strange death after his last battle of Camlann: he may not have died, but was borne away to the Isle of Avalon to be healed. Avalon has been identified with **Glastonbury**, but it may have been the Celtic Otherworld or the Isle of the Blest, where Arthur still lives. In his *Morte d'Arthur*, Sir Thomas Malory called Arthur *Rex quondam rexque futurus* – the Once and Future King.

In the centuries since this brave warrior battled against the Saxon foe and became a national folk-hero, a web of myth and legend has been woven around his life and exploits. **Camelot**, the Knights of the **Round Table**, the **Holy Grail** . . . all feature in the legends, and all have proved equally elusive in reality. But there are very many places throughout the British Isles claiming to be part of the Arthurian story. He was born at **Tintagel**; Camelot was on the **hillfort** of **South Cadbury Castle**; the Round Table was at Winchester, or Caerleon; his last battle, Camlann, was fought at Slaughter Bridge in Cornwall, or around Cader Idris in Snowdonia, or by the Somerset River Cam; the sword **Excalibur** was thrown into Dozmary Pool in Cornwall, or from Pomparles Bridge at Glastonbury; Arthur and his queen Guinevere were buried in Glastonbury Abbey (*see* **Glastonbury** for an account of the discovery of the grave).

There are legends in which Arthur has become a giant, sitting on mountain peaks, battling with other giants, playing quoits with the **Devil**; and there are many legendary locations for the cave where the king and his men still lie sleeping, awaiting the call to arise and help the nation in its time of need. These include

Alderley Edge in Cheshire, the **Eildon Hills** in Roxburgh, Craig-y-Ddinas in West Glamorgan, a cave beneath Richmond Castle in North Yorkshire and beneath the former Sewingshields Castle in Northumberland. Many more Arthurian sites are described in our book *The Enchanted Land*.

Astronomy

There is strong evidence that many ancient civilizations across the world studied the skies, and research at **stone circles** in Britain suggests that early scientists of the Late **Neolithic** and Early **Bronze Age** had considerable knowledge of astronomical events. Many circles incorporate alignments on the rising and setting **sun**, or the moon, or prominent stars. But it is not clear whether places like **Stonehenge** were constructed primarily as astronomical observatories, or whether the astronomical use was of secondary importance. It has been suggested that the astronomer-priests were an elite body with secret knowledge and that they used their insight into the movements of the heavenly bodies to retain their authority over the people. They might have seemed to be magically in control of the planets by apparently making them enter the **megalithic** monuments at preordained times: for example, the moon passes low over the horizon and so is seen among the stones at **Callanish** every 18½ years; also in Scotland, the moon appears to float along the flat stone in **recumbent stone circles** at certain times; at **Stonehenge** the **Midsummer** sun rises behind the Heel Stone; and at **Maes Howe** the midwinter sun shines into the inner chamber.

It might be possible that today we interpret early astronomy in terms of power because of the ethos of our own age. It is just as feasible that the astronomer-priests used their knowledge to harness natural energies we no longer understand, and that the stone circles were places where magical rituals were performed in order to utilize those energies. Without written records we cannot know how advanced or rudimentary was the astronomical knowledge of the Neolithic and Bronze Ages, or what they used that knowledge for, but it is clear that there were skilled astronomers, working without any of the equipment that is considered essential today, and achieving impressive results.

Recently archaeologists have excavated what appears to be ancient Europe's most sophisticated astronomical computer, a Neolithic temple at Godmanchester near Cambridge. It seems to have been designed to predict the major events of the year-long solar cycle and the 19-year lunar cycle, and may have been used as a temple for the worship of the sun and the moon. Twenty-four phallic wooden obelisks were arranged around the perimeter of the temple, perhaps the first forerunners of the maypole, that phallic symbol which was once an important feature of May Day celebrations. (*See also* **Energy; Phallus**.)

Avebury

Archaeologically known as a **henge**, like **Stonehenge** Avebury is an impressive site, though its impact is not so immediate. It consists of an open flat area surrounded by a bank nearly a mile round, and a ditch 9 metres (30 feet) deep. Inside the flat area are standing stones, the remains of **stone circles**: many of the stones were re-erected earlier this century, having been destroyed or buried in earlier centuries. In addition, a stone avenue extended for 2.5 kilometres (1½ miles) from the henge, and ended in a small stone circle known as The Sanctuary. A section of this, Kennet Avenue nearest to Avebury, has been restored: the stones average 3 metres (10 feet) in height and alternate in shape between tall, narrow stones and those of a broad lozenge or diamond shape, as do the stones in the Avebury circle. These shapes are thought to symbolize male and female. This, in addition to the fact that the avenue was serpentine in shape (and there may also have been another serpentine avenue leading in the opposite direction from Avebury), may be a pointer to the way in which the henge was used by the people who constructed it. The **serpent** symbolizes **energy**, and the people may have processed along the serpentine avenues generating energy as they moved towards the stone circles where, according to Michael Dames in his book *The Avebury Cycle*, they then engaged in powerful **fertility** rites in the Avebury Wedding Ring. Whether or not his interpretation is the correct one, the place was clearly very important: it has been calculated that one and a half million man-hours would have been required just to construct the enclosure. It equals the construction of the major cathedrals in later ages.

It is difficult to imagine how Avebury might have looked when it was in use, but the atmosphere there when ceremonies were being enacted, whatever their nature, must have been powerful. Tales of **ghosts** seen in the stones suggest that some of that power still remains. During the First World War, a writer of books about

Wiltshire, Edith Olivier, was driving through Avebury at twilight when she heard music and saw the lights of a fair among the stones. Later she learned that it was at least 50 years since a fair had been held there. On another occasion, many small figures were seen moving among the stones on a bright moonlit night, and the witness described the feeling as most uncanny.

Avebury is well worth a visit, preferably out of the tourist season when you can wander alone among the stones, and preferably when you have time to spend exploring the whole vast complex, which also includes **Silbury Hill**, another amazing prehistoric structure visible just across the fields from the Avebury henge.

Location: 9.5 kilometres (6 miles) W of Marlborough, Wiltshire. OS ref: SU 102699.

B

Bardsey Island
See **Isles, sacred**

Barrow

An earth mound covering a prehistoric burial. Barrows come in various shapes and sizes: long barrows were built in **Neolithic** times and usually covered a stone-built **burial chamber**; round barrows date from the later **Bronze Age** and contain a single burial. Other names describe the barrow shapes: bowl barrows, disc barrows, bell barrows, saucer barrows, etc. Tumulus is another name for a barrow, but if the mound was built of stone rather than earth, as often occurred in upland areas, the term **cairn** was used.

Bath

The Roman baths and temple-complex were built on the site of a much older sacred spring, which had been a cult centre in the **Iron Age**, and its name *Aquae Sulis* shows that the waters were dedicated to the native Celtic goddess Sulis, who was Minerva to the Romans. The surviving remains are very impressive, especially the Great Bath which is a large bathing pool fed with water from the sacred spring, and which would have been roofed over in Roman times. This is a hot spring, and the water in the bath steams gently, creating an air of mystery. When the bath and spring were cleaned out, many votive offerings were found, including jewellery, pewter vessels, and 12,000 coins – today people still throw coins into wishing wells. Also found were 90 curse-tablets made of lead, and inscribed with curses against people who had wronged the curser, usually by stealing something belonging to them. (*See also* **Holy wells**.)
Location: In Bath town centre, Avon. OS ref: ST 751647.

Black dogs

Black dogs may seem a strange subject for inclusion in a book on earth mysteries, but these black dogs are not harmless family pets – they are phantom hounds from hell! They are also very place-orientated: they haunt certain stretches of road, especially ancient trackways; they also frequent churchyards and **prehistoric sites**. Their presence in such locations suggests that they may have some link with the **ley** phenomenon, a link we explored in our book *Alien Animals*.

Black dogs are not wholly legendary: people still see them today. In one common form of the story, the large, friendly animal appears from nowhere to escort a woman travelling alone along a dark rural road. It is convincingly substantial until she puts out a hand to pat her welcome companion . . . and feels nothing at all! There have been reports of such guardians protecting women from lurking vagabonds who have been deterred by the sight of such seemingly real animals. Yet sometimes the ghostly dogs appear to be omens of death and disaster, and as such are not at all welcome to those who see them unexpectedly.

Over the centuries phantom black dogs have been seen in all parts of the British Isles, and are usually distinguishable from living dogs by their large size, shaggy coat, huge fiery eyes, and their behaviour. One of the most famous is Black Shuck of East Anglia, an area particularly rich in black dog lore. At the height of a terrible storm on the morning of Sunday 4 August 1577, a black dog suddenly appeared in the churches at Bungay and Blythburgh in Suffolk. His presence was fatal, for he passed between two members of the congregation as they knelt in prayer and they both died. He left his calling-card at Blythburgh, where claw-like marks can still be seen scorched on to one of the church doors. At Bungay, the event is commemorated in the design of a weather vane in the town centre, which features a black dog.

Bleeding trees
See **Nevern; Trees**

Bonfires
See **Fire ceremonies**

Boundaries

Although we are scarcely aware of them, territorial boundaries are all around us: from country boundaries, county boundaries, parish boundaries, down to our own personal boundaries like the garden fence or our bedroom walls. Although area boundaries are invisible to us today, existing mainly on maps, in earlier times before maps existed, boundaries were clearly marked on the ground so that all were aware of them. Linear earthworks such as Offa's Dyke and Wansdyke were boundary markers, with the deep ditches and high banks giving them an added role as a defensive earthwork if the need arose. Although difficult to prove now, it is possible that some **prehistoric sites** such as **barrows** and other **burial chambers** also served a dual function as boundary markers. Isolated **standing stones** and **crosses** could also have been used in this way.

Ancient boundaries are not just prosaic historical features: they also have a mysterious component. There are places in the countryside that have a special feel about them, an atmosphere that is hard to describe, and they often turn out to be points on an ancient boundary. Why this should be so, we cannot determine. It is illustrated by research into **black dogs**, those mysterious phantoms that have a long pedigree of haunting Britain's lanes. They seem drawn to ancient trackways and boundaries, with a tendency to patrol set routes. One example of this is a green lane at Uplyme in Devon, which follows the route of the county boundary, and is also haunted by a black dog, after whom an adjoining inn has been named.

The importance of boundaries is also shown by the old Rogationtide (fifth week after Easter) custom of Beating the Bounds, when a group of people from the parish would walk round the boundaries, with the priest preaching or offering prayers at certain points along the route. Young boys would be bumped against boundary marker stones, made to wade through streams and ponds, over walls and hedges, even over houses, where a boundary crossed them, to impress the route of the boundary upon them. This custom also incorporated a blessing on the fields, so in that respect was a link with ancient **fertility** rituals.

Bride
Bride was a **fertility** goddess worshipped by the **Celts**: she was in fact a triple goddess, who became the Christian St Brigid/Brigit/Bridget/Bride, and was widely revered in Scotland and Ireland. In the Scottish Highlands women in labour sought Bride's help in bringing about an easy delivery. She also brought life to the dead

winter, and her day was 1 February, which was when the ancient pagan Celtic festival of Imbolc was held. On the eve of St Bride's Day, girls used to make and decorate corn dollies which they took to each household. Everyone had to give a small present to Bride, and special cakes were baked. After a procession the girls celebrated with feasting and dancing. The older women made straw cradles or baskets called Bride's Bed. An image of Bride made of oats was placed inside and a wooden wand was given to her. If next morning the marks of this wand could be seen in the ashes on the hearth, that was a good omen for the coming year.

Brigantia, the 'High One', was probably also the same as Bride. Brigantia was the goddess of the Brigantes, who were a tribe living in northern England or Brigantia; a carved figure of her 1 metre (3 feet) high was found at the Roman fort of Blatobulgium (Birrens) in Dumfriesshire.

Broch

A dry-stone tower with rooms and staircases in the hollow walls which were 3.5-4.5 metres (12-15 feet) thick. Brochs were built as defensive homesteads late in the **Iron Age**, and are mostly found in northern and western Scotland, where the remains of more than 500 have been identified. The best are superbly built, at the peak of British drystone architecture in prehistoric times, and several impressive examples still survive, the best probably being **Mousa broch** in the Shetland Islands.

Bronze Age

The Bronze Age in Britain lasted over 1,000 years, from around 2000 BC, and was so named because bronze was used for making tools. It ended when iron came into use, and the **Iron Age** began. Many of the **prehistoric sites** we can still see today were constructed in the Bronze Age, such as round **barrows, cairns, stone circles** and **standing stones**.

Burial chamber

A prehistoric tomb, usually taking the form of a central chamber built of large stone slabs, roofed with a huge capstone, and then covered by a mound of earth (**barrow** or **tumulus**) or stone (**cairn**). If the covering mound has disappeared, the exposed stone structure is known as a dolmen, cromlech or quoit. There are many good examples still to be seen in Britain, for example **Lanyon**

Quoit, West Kennet Long Barrow, Pentre Ifan, Cairnholy chambered cairns and **Maes Howe**.

It is generally assumed that these structures were simply burial chambers and had no other function, but the best surviving examples are so impressive that the possibility of other uses must be considered. They may have been used for rituals or ceremonies, in the same way that our churches and cathedrals were used for both ceremonies and burials. There are a few earth or stone mounds in Britain that remain a total enigma, one well-known example being **Silbury Hill** in Wiltshire. Truly huge in size, archaeological excavations have failed to find any trace of a burial inside it. Equally puzzling but less well known is **Gop Cairn** in Clwyd, 12 metres (40 feet) high and surpassed only by Silbury Hill.

C

Cadbury
See **South Cadbury Castle**

Cairn
A prehistoric stone-built **burial chamber**, or single burial, with a covering of stones rather than earth is called a cairn. *See also* **Clava cairns** and **Kilmartin cairn cemetery**.

Cairnholy chambered cairns
Two **Neolithic burial chambers** in a beautiful location above Wigtown Bay, both with impressive upright stones.
Location: N of A75 between Newton Stewart and Gatehouse of Fleet, Kirkcudbright. Not easy to find, but can be reached by car; best to use OS map. OS ref: NX 517538.

Callanish
This is one of Britain's major prehistoric sites, perhaps second only to **Stonehenge**, but because of its remote location on an island off Scotland, not nearly so closely studied as Stonehenge. A stone avenue, stone rows, and a **stone circle** form a cross shape; a 4.6 metre (15-foot) **standing stone** is at the centre. The stones were all erected during the **Bronze Age**, but the date of a chambered round **cairn** in the circle is uncertain. Each generation has tried to interpret this enigmatic site, and it has been seen as a Temple of the **Druids**, a site of sun worship, an early calendar, and a sundial with the standing stone as the pointer. More recently, astronomical survey work has shown that Callanish is orientated towards the year's major solar events. This is echoed in a folklore belief that at sunrise on Midsummer Day the 'Shining One' would walk along the avenue, his arrival announced by the cuckoo's cry. The moon's cycle seems also to have been of importance, with especially dramatic events taking place every 18½ years when the moon passes low over the

horizon and appears to be actually among the stones. This happened in 1987 and will again in 2006. Viewed from Callanish at the crucial time, the moon appears to rise out of the Pairc Hills, known as The Sleeping Beauty because they resemble a woman lying on her back: the **Earth Mother** giving birth, perhaps?

In the past, the Gaelic name *Fir Bhreig* (false men) was used for the stones, as they looked like human figures from a distance. There was also a legend that they were giants turned to stone (*see* **Petrifaction**) by St Kieran for failing to embrace Christianity when he came and preached to them. It was at one time customary for men and women to exchange betrothal vows among the stones, and even to consummate their marriages there to ensure a happy future: the stones were clearly regarded as a place which promoted **fertility**.

Location: On the Island of Lewis in the Western Isles, 21 kilometres (13 miles) W of Stornoway. OS ref: NB 214331.

Camelot

In medieval romance this was King **Arthur's** main dwelling place, but its true location is never made clear, so various guesses have been made based on what the chroniclers said, and the places suggested include London, Colchester, Winchester, Carlisle, Camelford, Caerleon and Caerwent. But the favoured location is **South Cadbury Castle** in Somerset.

Camlann

See **Arthur, King**

Carn Euny settlement and fogou

The remains of prehistoric stone huts (probably dating from the first century BC) can be seen here, with hearths, postholes and drains, but the most impressive structure is the **fogou**, an underground stone-built chamber. Fogous may have been used for purely domestic purposes – food storage, hiding place – or they may have been used for rituals and ceremonies of a religious or magical nature. At one end of the Carn Euny fogou is a well-preserved circular stone chamber. Carn Euny fogou was one of the locations for the **Dragon Project dream research** programme. There is another impressive prehistoric village not far away at Chysauster (5 kilometres (3 miles) north of Penzance).

Location: 6.5 kilometres (4 miles) WSW of Penzance, Cornwall. OS ref: SW 402288.

Carvings in churches

Older churches are often very rich in strange carvings, some of the work being very fine indeed. The meaning of some of the carvings is controversial: were they purely decorative, or did they hold a message for the onlooker, either a warning, or some esoteric knowledge? The sort of carvings we refer to include **exhibitionists**, **green men**, **dragons**, some or all of which may have a **fertility** link; and also, less obviously, 'tongue-pokers' – grotesque faces with protruding tongues. These were once thought to signify death by hanging, but later it was suggested that they were fertility symbols, the tongue being the **phallus**. In one carving (Willingham, Cambridgeshire), the large protruding tongue covers the genital region. Also, the 'rude' action of sticking one's tongue out may be linked to the 'tongue as phallus' symbolism. Another style of carving with sexual overtones is the 'mouth-puller' where a grotesque figure uses its hands to pull open its mouth – a gesture which closely parallels the female exhibitionist pulling open her vulva.

Castlerigg stone circle

One of the most impressively-sited **prehistoric sites** in Britain. Thirty-eight stones stand in a circle 30 metres (100 feet) in diameter, set in a natural amphitheatre in the Cumbrian hills. The mystery is, why were these stones set out here? **Stone circles** may have been built for ceremonial purposes, or for early scientific experiments. A researcher investigating shadow paths found that the tallest stone at Castlerigg casts a long shadow at sunset on the summer solstice. At Candlemas (2 February) the shadow points to the sunrise, and it seems feasible to suggest that the stones were used to make astronomical calculations (*see* **Astronomy**).

Two men passing close to the stones one night earlier this century saw white lights moving around within the circle. One light came straight towards them, but went out before it reached them. Mystery lights seen at prehistoric sites are certainly a natural phenomenon of some kind, like ball lightning (*see* **Earth lights**), but if such sites seem to attract such natural outbursts of **energy**, perhaps that was why circles were built there, so that the energies could be used in some way? Pure speculation, but all possibilities must be considered in the search for the reasons why our ancestors went to such great lengths to build circles of stones. It would have been much easier to make circles of wooden stakes, if they simply needed to delineate an area of ground as a ritual site, but they fetched huge rocks and set them into specially dug holes. Granite is often found at such sites, as is **quartz**, which suggests that the presence of certain rocks was important for the correct functioning of the circle.

Location: 2.5 kilometres (1½ miles) E of Keswick, Cumbria. OS ref: NY 292237.

Caves

The cave can be seen as the womb of the **Earth Mother**, its downward and inward-looking nature being definitely female, as contrasted with the outward and upward-pointing masculine mountain. Equally the cave can be a grave, and an entrance into the Underworld or Otherworld, the place of the dead, or the home of the **fairies**. Rituals and ceremonies were performed in caves (as shown by the ancient cave-paintings found in several locations abroad), and it is probable that **Neolithic** stone structures which are now classified as **burial chambers**, such as **barrows**, also had other functions and were used for rituals in the same way as caves. The surviving **megalithic** tombs, with their inner chambers constructed of large stone slabs, are very similar to caves. (*See* **Maes Howe passage grave**; **West Kennet long barrow**.) **Underground passages** often began in caves; and treasure was hidden there, guarded by **dragons** and other frightening monsters. Folk-heroes sometimes took refuge in caves, and some of them were even said to lie asleep in caves, waiting for the call to come to the aid of their countrymen. The most famous sleeping hero is of course King **Arthur** who, impossibly, sleeps in several caves in Britain, including one in Craig-y-Ddinas rock in West Glamorgan, South Wales. Details of other sleeping heroes, and much more cave folklore, can be found in our book *The Enchanted Land*.

Celts

A mysterious group of people who came into Britain from central Europe, and also left archaeological traces in France, Spain, north Italy, and other places. The Gauls were Celts (Gaul is now France). Their earliest archaeological remains date back to 1300 BC in the Upper Danube region, and among other victories they sacked Rome and Delphi, but when the Romans became powerful and expanded their territory, the Celts were pushed north and west, and finally settled in Brittany, western Britain and Ireland. They have left an important cultural legacy, which includes the Gaelic, Welsh and Breton languages, all still spoken today. Their art was also of major importance, some of the best examples being created in Britain. They left behind bronze food vessels and weapons, gold ornaments, and other items, all ornately decorated, and also stone objects including **crosses**, again highly decorated, usually with Christian themes, because Celtic Christianity has left a lasting impression in western Britain and Ireland. The Celtic culture was complex, and many books have been written about them, their beliefs and their mythology, as well as about the treasures they have left us.

Cerne Abbas Giant

One of Britain's finest **hill figures**, the 55 metre (180-foot) tall **giant** lies on his back just outside the Dorset village after which he is named. His outline was cut into the white chalk many centuries ago, possibly as long as the 2nd century AD, but who he was intended to represent is uncertain. Perhaps he was the pagan god Hercules; but whoever he was, the naked figure with erect phallus and knobbed club held threateningly above his head, was looked upon as a source of **fertility**. It was the custom for barren women to sit on the figure, presumably on the phallus itself as being the most relevant part of the giant's anatomy, though some people believed that in order to cure barrenness, the man and woman should have sexual intercourse on the giant. On aerial photographs of the figure, a small earth enclosure can be made out above his head. This was known as the Frying Pan or the Trendle, and on 30 April a firwood maypole used to be erected annually, ready for the **May Day** festivities. Such celebrations were originally fertility rituals, and the maypole itself can be thought of as a giant **phallus**. A **ley** passes through the Trendle and other antiquities at Cerne Abbas, though not through the giant himself. (Full details can be found in Paul Devereux's book *The New Ley Hunter's Guide*.)

Location: 8 kilometres (5 miles) N of Dorchester, Dorset. OS ref: ST 666017.

Chalice Well

The water in this **Glastonbury** well is reddish in colour because of its high iron content, and it is probably this which gave rise to the belief that the **Holy Grail**, containing Christ's blood, was hidden in the well. (*See also* **Holy wells**.)

Location: In a garden open to the public at the foot of Glastonbury Tor, Somerset. OS ref: ST 507385.

Christmas

Now known as a celebration of the birth of Christ, this festival is much older than Christianity. Falling at the time of the winter solstice (22 December, the shortest day of the year), it marks the point when the days again begin to lengthen, and spring is in sight. The arrival of spring was encouraged by the lighting of bonfires, by burning the Yule Log, by decorating the house with greenery, and burning lights on a Christmas tree. (*See also* **Fire ceremonies**.)

Churches

The earliest stone churches were built from the 7th century onwards, though few traces of these remain. Saxon churches dating from the 10th century are the earliest that can now be seen. But it is clear that very often, churches were built on sites that were sacred in earlier times. This may simply have been because the church founder was aware of the geomantic properties of the site and wished to utilize them; or possibly the intention was to negate and supplant the pagan energies which were linked to the place, and to use an already established centre of ritual gatherings. Whatever the reason, there is clear evidence of continuity of use. Some churches have prehistoric **standing stones** in the churchyard, as at **Rudston** which has Britain's tallest standing stone close to the church, and Midmar in Aberdeen which has a **recumbent stone circle** in the churchyard. Others were built inside earthworks, as at **Knowlton** where there is a ruined church inside a **henge**, or Cholesbury (Buckinghamshire) where the church was built inside a **hillfort**. Sometimes churches were even built on top of burial mounds, as were the two medieval chapels constructed on the **Neolithic** burial mound of La Hougue Bie in Jersey.

Legends telling of partly built churches being mysteriously moved to other sites overnight may refer to conflict within the church community over the best place to build the church, perhaps some disagreement between those who supported older, pagan-rooted practices, and those who wished to eradicate them. Or maybe the legends hold memories of esoteric practices such as divination or **dowsing**, once used to select the most favourable site in order to make best use of the earth energies. Some churches are undoubtedly alive with **energy**, which can sometimes be sensed as a humming sound, or a sensation inside your head. The building may focus natural energies present at the site, which can be beneficially used by the worshippers there.

Possible evidence of pagan beliefs can also be detected in mysterious **carvings** in some churches: **green men, dragons, exhibitionists**, etc.

Circle

A universal symbol which has featured in all major religions. A wheel-cross (circle enclosing cross) symbolized the four seasons, the four ages of man, the four quarters of the earth, and also Paradise with four rivers coming from the central Tree of Life. On the ground it can be seen where a circular churchyard encloses a cross-shaped church. At **Old Sarum**, a circular prehistoric hillfort encloses a church; so too does the prehistoric **henge** at **Knowlton**. Circles were also made of stones in prehistoric times (*see* **Stone circles**), and carved on to rock (*see* **Cup and ring marks**).

Clava cairns

Three stone **cairns**, probably built during the **Neolithic** period, have been encircled by **stone circles**, many hundreds or even a thousand or two years later, in the **Bronze Age**. In all ages, people have adopted and reused the holy sites of their forebears; it has happened comparatively recently, with Christian **churches** being built on **prehistoric sites**. (*See* **Knowlton Circles** *and* **Rudston Monolith**.) Several more thousand years later, we can only guess at the motivations of our ancestors, but in the case of Clava it is possible that the site once had an astronomical function. Professor Alexander Thom, who surveyed many prehistoric sites and made many interesting discoveries concerning their geometry, found an alignment at Clava that pointed to the midwinter **sun's** setting position. So many prehistoric sites embody evidence for early **astronomy**, and it is likely that the astronomer-priests of the time were far more knowledgeable than is generally acknowledged today.

Location: Near Culloden battlefield, 9.5 kilometres (6 miles) E of Inverness. OS ref: NH 757445.

Cock-crow stones

Some **standing stones** were said to be able to turn round every time the cock crew, such as the Cock-Crow Stone at Wellington

(Somerset). It was at this time that you might be lucky enough to see the **treasure** lying under the stone. The topmost stone of the Cheesewring on Bodmin Moor (Cornwall) is another that turns three times when it hears the cock crow – note the important word 'hears', showing that this may be some kind of rural joke, since stones are not able (so far as we know) to hear. Other stones are said to turn over when the clock strikes twelve, or when they *hear* the clock strike. More examples are given in our book *The Secret Country (see also **Moving stones**).

Countless stones

Some **stone circles** have a belief attached to them that it is impossible to count the stones twice and get the same total. One of the methods used to try to overcome this was to place a small loaf of bread on each stone, and this was tried at the **Rollright Stones**, **Stonehenge**, and **The Hurlers**, among others. One site was even named from this tradition: The Countless Stones (or Lower Kit's Coty House) in Kent. But even the ingenious loaf system failed, and several reasons were given: either the baker ran out of loaves, or a loaf was missing each time he counted, or the **Devil** ate some of the loaves, or the baker dropped dead just when he was ready to announce his total. Perhaps the loaf tradition was a memory of the once-frequent custom of leaving **offerings** at **sacred sites**.

Coventina's Well

Although not much can be seen of the well today, other than some marshy ground, this was once an important Roman well, sacred to the Celtic goddess Coventina, and enclosed in a square temple. Excavation has revealed many intriguing objects: votive offerings including more than 14,000 Roman coins, bronze animals and heads, pottery, bells, glass, part of a human skull (possible **head-cult** links?), several large altars, some bearing images of the goddess, and pins which suggest that **fertility** and **healing** were sought here. (*See also* **Holy wells**.) This site should be compared with the sacred springs at **Bath**.

There are the ruins of another temple close by, where the Lord of Light, Mithras, was worshipped in a male-only mystery cult. Although this Mithraeum was destroyed in the 4th century, dates on the coins show that the well was in use into the 5th century. Five Mithraea have been found in Britain: they were built either close to streams or actually over springs, but the significance of **water** in the cult of Mithras, a god of Persian and Zoroastrian origin, is not clear. Interestingly, the temple contained a statue of a Celtic **mother goddess**.

Location: Close to the Roman fort of Carrawburgh on Hadrian's Wall, Northumberland. OS ref: NY 857711.

Cromlech

A term from Wales, used to describe prehistoric **burial chambers** built from large stone slabs and covered by a huge capstone; also sometimes (though not usually today) applied to **stone circles**. Virtually interchangeable with **dolmen** and **quoit**.

Crop circles

Corn circles or crop circles are an example of a phenomenon that has sprung up in recent years, rather than having been known of for hundreds of years, as is usually the case. This sudden development is in itself a cause for suspicion. Also suspicious is the way the phenomenon has changed during the 1980s and into the 1990s. At first the circles were simply that: plain circles of flattened corn, usually in the large cornfields of southern England. Then the patterns gradually became more complex, and the theories which had been devised to explain the simple circles – unusual winds or even a plasma vortex – were seen to be unlikely, because they could not explain the multiplicity of formations which were now being discovered. The phenomenon also spread to other parts of Britain, and people began to come forward and admit to having made crop circles. Many enthusiasts were dubious about these confessions: the circles were so good, and why was no one ever caught? So the makers gave demonstrations, but still the enthusiasts refused to believe them, preferring to call upon more esoteric creators, such as **UFOs**, aliens, the spirit of the earth, the Great Mother, etc., their motivation being concern that time is running out for humanity, unless we learn to take better care of our planet. The sentiments are fine, but the proof is lacking, and there is a much simpler explanation on hand: that the formations really are being made by human beings. They are in fact a form of landscape art, skilfully created through the use of human ingenuity.

Cross

Although now known as a Christian symbol, the cross predates Christianity and has had many symbolic meanings down the ages.

It was used on **Bronze Age** burial artefacts some 4,000 years ago; the Egyptian ankh was a cross; to the New Zealand Maoris the cross was the moon goddess; to the Maya the tau cross was the Tree of Life; and so on.

Not all crosses have arms. Some old Christian crosses are decidedly phallic in appearance, being just a tall shaft ending in a rounded knob (*see* **Phallus**), and these may have developed from prehistoric **standing stones**. Sometimes standing stones have been Christianized by having crosses carved on them, or being shaped into a rough cross, and many examples of these can be found in Cornwall. The cross with arms has been compared to a tree, and thus is a symbol of **fertility**: in a 16th-century engraving the crucified Christ hangs on a cross bearing leaves and fruit, symbolizing the fecundity of sacrifice. Many Christian crosses in Britain are carved with elaborate patterns and Christian themes, especially the Celtic crosses found mainly in Wales, and the Saxon crosses found in the north of England. St Brynach's Cross at **Nevern** in Dyfed is a fine example: 4 metres (13 feet) high, it is covered with intricate Celtic interlace. The cross was also used as a symbol to keep evil away, tiny crosses being carved on church buildings and elsewhere.

Crossroads

The point where two or more roads cross has long been considered a special place, haunted by mysterious beings – **ghosts, fairies,** demons, witches – and the place where strange phenomena happen. **Healing** rites were performed there, also divination and prophecy and other magical practices. Gallows were set up at crossroads, and suicides and murderers were buried there, possibly in order to confuse the restless spirits and stop them wandering. Crossings of ancient tracks are often found along the line of **leys,** and **markstones** were often located at crossroads.

Crystals

Stones in **stone circles** are often found to consist partly of crystals, especially **quartz**. This may have been because of the electrical properties in crystals, and their power to affect human consciousness. Numerous people have experienced strange sensations when touching **standing stones,** including being thrown back from them. Some experiments were done with crystals as part of the **Dragon Project**, as described in Paul Devereux's book *Places of*

Power. In recent years the use of crystals in healing has become a feature of New Age beliefs and practices, and some people have even buried crystals at ancient **sacred sites** in order to 'adjust' the **energies** there. This dangerous practice cannot be condoned, as the superficial knowledge of these self-appointed guardians does not allow them to know what they are doing, nor to be aware of the disruption which they might cause to a site's energy patterns.

Cup and ring marks

These are prehistoric rock carvings, consisting of a central depression or cup, surrounded by concentric circles. They are widely found on exposed rocks in certain parts of the country, especially northern England and Scotland, and they are also found on stones at **prehistoric sites** such as **stone circles**, **standing stones**, etc. There are many other designs, more or less complex than the basic cup and ring, and they are thought to date from the **Bronze Age**, but their meaning and purpose are unknown. Many explanations (over 100!) have been put forward, including magical symbols (representations of parts of the **mother goddess's** body, **fertility** symbols, etc.), route markers, written messages, marks made by early copper and gold prospectors, water diviners' symbols, cups for blood **sacrifices**, maps of the countryside or the stars, **boundary** markers, and so on. As early man seems to have been concerned with the movements of the stars and planets, judging by the surviving evidence for an early form of **astronomy**, it seems possible that the rock carvings had an astronomical function, perhaps being used in a magical ritual to bring back the often-absent **sun**, so vital to the wellbeing of the people.

But comparison with earlier rock carvings may also be informative: there are in France some carvings dating from the Upper Palaeolithic period (which dates from around 38,000 BC to around 8000 BC, very roughly) which clearly depict the female vulva. We do not of course know why they were carved, other than that people have always been preoccupied with the encouragement of fertility, but it is possible that they played a part in rituals and ceremonies designed to promote fertility. It is also possible that in later times (the cup and ring marks were carved at least 6,000 years after the vulvas, and possibly much longer afterwards) stylized vulvas were carved, which appeared as simple hollows in the rock. Most probably the simple cup marks and more elaborate cup and ring marks had a variety of meanings and functions, which we can only guess at today.

Cursus

The name means 'race-course' and comes from the Latin; it was given to these enigmatic prehistoric earthworks in the 18th century by the antiquarian researcher William Stukeley, who thought that was what they must have been. In fact they date from the **Neolithic** period, and their purpose is not nearly so clear-cut as Stukeley believed. The cursus consists of a long avenue bounded by parallel earth banks with ditches outside. There is one at **Stonehenge** nearly 3 kilometres (2 miles) long, the first one to be identified, but the longest is the Dorset cursus, nearly 9.5 kilometres (6 miles) long. They form long straight lines across the landscape, often incorporating burial mounds, and Paul Devereux has suggested that they represent **spirit lines** (see his book *Lines on the Landscape*). Dr G.T. Meaden has also investigated cursuses, and in his book *The Stonehenge Solution* links them to the tracks followed by tornadoes. The cursus was the path along which the Sky God travelled in the guise of a tornado. The phallic shape of the tornado as seen in the sky represented the Sky God's **phallus**, and the cursus was 'dedicated to the Divine or Sacred Marriage'.

Customs

Many of the traditional customs that are still practised in Britain may be the last remnants of rituals practised hundreds or even several thousand years ago, when the people were closer to the natural cycles of nature than we are today, and were very concerned to promote the **fertility** of the land, their crops and animals, and of the people themselves. In winter, **fire ceremonies** were held on certain key days, such as **Samhain**, the start of the Celtic year: 31 October, or Hallowe'en. Also at the winter solstice, or 22 December, the shortest day of the year, when the high point was the bringing in of the Yule log. After several days' burning, the remains were used in various ways to help fertilize earth, crops and cattle.

At **Easter** the return of spring was celebrated, with eggs symbolizing rebirth, re-creation and immortality. The high point of all the spring festivals was **May Day**, when the fertility of the earth was reaffirmed and celebrated in various ways. Dancing round a phallic maypole was one way, and foliage-clad figures like **Jack-in-the-Green** who came out at this time were striking reminders of the coming of new life. At harvest-time in the autumn, various rituals celebrated the completion of a successful growing season, and in earlier times the whole agricultural cycle was accompanied by rituals to promote fertility: ashes from purifying bonfires were scattered, blood-letting was performed (perhaps a relic of earlier ritual **sacrifices**?), crop growth rituals like Beating the Bounds and wassailing were performed.

The fact that so many traditional customs are still practised today, even though very few people are aware of the significance of the rituals they are performing, demonstrates the instinctive appeal they make to the human psyche. Just a few examples of still surviving customs are: the Padstow 'Obby' Oss festivities on May Day (*see* **Horse**); the Haxey Hood Game which takes place on 6 January (Old Christmas Day) in Lincolnshire and may be the remains of a pagan fertility rite; the **Up-Helly-Aa** fire-festival held at Lerwick in the Shetlands at the end of January; and the **Abbots Bromley Horn Dance** held in September in a Staffordshire village, where the participants wear antlers – the dance may link back to pre-Christian fertility magic.

Another possible link between a long-standing traditional custom and the ritual practices of prehistory has come to light with the excavation of a **Neolithic** astronomical temple at Godmanchester near Cambridge. Twenty-four phallic wooden obelisks stood around the perimeter of the temple, the two largest facing the place where the **sun** rose on May Day, and it has been suggested that the obelisks were the earliest forerunners of the maypole. (*See* **Phallus**.)

Cynwch, Llyn

Llyn Cynwch is one of North Wales's many beautiful lakes, set in breathtaking countryside yet easily accessible on foot. Few visitors to this picturesque spot, however, are aware of the interesting folklore which surrounds the lake. It is one of several lakes in the area whose indwelling water spirit was said to periodically claim a human victim. It was believed that on New Year's Eve the spirit took human form and could be seen walking back and forth along the lake shore, crying in Welsh: 'The hour is come, but not the man!'

According to folklore, one man did go into the lake and emerge alive. He was a servant at Nannau, the big house nearby, who one day fell into the water, but didn't drown. As he sank, he found the water getting clearer, until he landed on the bottom where he found people and places as though they were on dry land. A short, fat old man asked him what he was doing there. He was made welcome and stayed for about a month, although it seemed to him like three days. His hosts took him along an **underground passage** which led up under the hearthstone of another local house where his sweetheart worked. Clearly Llyn Cynwch is also one of several Welsh lakes in which the fairyfolk are still believed to dwell. (*See* **Fairies.**)

Another belief was that a deadly viper or serpent once lived by the lake and that any living creature that was caught by its eye became helplessly transfixed. One day, a shepherd took advantage of finding it asleep, fetched an axe and killed it. A cairn of stones was piled over its carcase and named Carnedd y Wiber (Cairn of the Viper).

Location: On the route of the Precipice Walk, starting 4 kilometres (2½ miles) N of Dolgellau, Gwynedd. Car park OS ref: SH 745211.

D

Devil

Many natural landscape features in Britain were formed by giants, according to folklore, but the Devil also played a considerable part. He threw huge rocks around (*see* **Rudston monolith** and **Devil's Arrows**), often trying to demolish Christian churches, and he dug out **caves** and caverns, but he wasn't all-powerful, and in one lovely story he was outwitted by an old woman. On this occasion he decided to dig a channel through the South Downs in Sussex, in order to let the sea in and drown all the people who were converting to Christianity and building a lot of churches. As he dug, the earth from his spade was flung around him, forming hills like Chanctonbury, Cissbury and Mount Caburn. He was working fast to get the task finished before daylight, but he was making rather a noise, and an old woman in a cottage close by woke up and saw what he was doing. She put a candle in her window, with a sieve in front so that it looked like the rising sun, and she also knocked her cockerel off his perch so that he crowed. The Devil heard this, and saw what he thought was the sun coming up, so he hurriedly flew off, a lump of earth dropping from his cloven hoof and forming the Isle of Wight. The unfinished ditch he was digging became known as the Devil's Dyke. Many more examples of the Devil's handiwork can be found in our book *The Enchanted Land*.

The Devil so hated by the Christians, with his horns and cloven hoofs, was also the pagan **horned god** of **fertility**. The cult of the horned god was widespread among the **Celts** in Europe and Britain, and he was frequently depicted in carvings and metal-work, with antlers, bull's horns or ram's horns. In all cases he was understood to be a bringer of fertility and this aspect was empha-sized especially in Brigantia in the north-east of Britain, where horned figures with **phallus** have been found. The rites of the horned god were widely practised and of great antiquity when the Christian missionaries were spreading across Europe, and they

25

saw it as their duty to suppress and discredit the old gods in order to promote the new. So the pagan horned god was turned into the Devil, a hated symbol of evil.

Devil's Arrows

These are three impressive **standing stones** 5.5-6.8 metres (18-22 ½ feet) tall set roughly in a line 174 metres (570 feet) long, though there was once a fourth, pulled down probably in the 16th century by people seeking **treasure**. The stone is millstone grit, quarried at Knaresborough 10.5 kilometres (6½ miles) away: how on earth were the stones transported to their present site? Folklore answers this question: they were thrown here by the **Devil**. His aim was to destroy a Christian settlement at Aldborough, and he fired four arrows from Howe Hill near Fountains Abbey, but they all fell short.

The St Barnabas Fair was held near the stones in centuries past, possibly a memory of the ceremonies which were held here several thousand years ago, when the stones were newly erected. Clearly they weren't erected on a whim, but for an important reason. Does the fact that they are almost in a line hold a clue to this reason? Perhaps it had something to do with prehistoric **astronomy**, or maybe the stones formed an early **ley** alignment. In his book *The New Ley Hunter's Guide* Paul Devereux found the Devil's Arrows to be on an 8-kilometre (5-mile) ley, aligning with two **henges** and a **tumulus**.
Location: At Boroughbridge near Ripon, North Yorkshire. OS ref: SE 391665.

Dinas Bran

This prominent Welsh hill may be an important site in Arthurian legend. Its name means Bran's Stronghold, Bran being a king of Britain and the hero of a *Mabinogion* tale. He was killed following an invasion of Ireland and his head was buried in the White Hill, believed to be Tower Hill in London. So long as the head remained buried, this island was protected against invasion; but King **Arthur** had the head exhumed, since he wished to protect the island through his strength alone. 'Bran' means raven, and the story of his buried head is thought to be connected with the belief that the presence of ravens at the Tower keeps the country safe from invasion. There might also be an echo of the ancient Celtic **head-cult**: severed heads were kept as talismans, and stone heads were carved to represent guardian deities. Dinas Bran also has other Arthurian links, and more than once it has been suggested that the hill was the hiding place of the mystical **Holy Grail**. According to folklore, a golden harp is said to be hidden in the hill, but it can only be found by a boy who has a white dog with a silver eye: such dogs were said to be able to see the wind.

Dinas Bran was also said to be a haunt of the **fairies**, and a young lad watching sheep was caught up into a fairy dance on the hillside. The musician turned into the **Devil**, and the boy couldn't stop dancing, until found and rescued by his master. Today the ruins of an **Iron Age hillfort** and medieval castle crown the hilltop.

Location: Outside Llangollen, Clwyd. OS ref: SJ 222430.

Dinas Emrys

This rocky, tree-covered hill in Snowdonia might not merit a second glance as you drive past, but it is an atmospheric place with an important legendary history. It is the site of a prehistoric **hillfort**, but not just any old hillfort: this one was said to have been built by King Vortigern who was seeking a place of refuge from the Saxons. He called in his magicians for assistance when the building kept falling down, and they advised that he should sacrifice a fatherless boy and sprinkle his blood on the site. A boy who fitted their description was found in south Wales at Carmarthen: this was the young **Merlin**. He saved his own life by telling Vortigern that the cause of the problem was two **dragons** who were in a pool under the hilltop. One was white, representing the Saxons, and the other was red, representing the Britons, and the two were fighting. He went on to make further prophecies, which came true. King Vortigern left Dinas Emrys and went elsewhere for sanctuary, the hillfort being taken over by Merlin, who buried his **treasure** there in a **cave**. He said that it would be found by a fair-haired, blue-eyed youth, and when the right person approaches the cave will open to the ringing of bells. We do not recommend searching for the cave, because the hill is steep, rocky, wooded and therefore inaccessible. But it can be viewed from the road which passes beneath it.

Location: 3 kilometres (2 miles) NE of Beddgelert, Gwynedd, beside A498. OS ref: SH 605492.

Divining
See **Dowsing**

Dolmen

Often used to describe a **burial chamber** that consists of large stone slabs topped by a capstone, the whole originally covered with earth; sometimes called a portal dolmen. Interchangeable with **cromlech** and **quoit**. A fine example with a well-balanced capstone is **Pentre Ifan**. The modern eye sees the balance of the stones as aesthetically pleasing. But did the tomb builders view it in this way, or were they simply building to a traditional design, with form following purpose? Probably the latter is true, especially if, as is believed today, the stone structure was hidden under an earth mound.

Dowsing

Although many people connect dowsing with water divining, today its applications are much wider. Dowsing has been used in archaeological research since at least the 1930s, the best-known dowser in this field being Guy Underwood who published *The Pattern of the Past* describing his work. To the uninitiated, his water lines, track lines, aquastats, blind springs, primary spirals, nodes, branch spirals and other subdivisions of the 'geodetic lines' he traced with his divining rod are difficult to comprehend, but some of his findings concerning the 'Earth Force' may be relevant to the study of earth mysteries.

Following much intensive dowsing at **prehistoric sites**, **churches** and cathedrals, Underwood concluded that the positions and layouts of such sites were actually determined by the geodetic lines to be found there. He worked solely with underground patterns, whereas later dowsers have located effects above ground. **Standing stones** have been found to carry **energy** charges which are sometimes so powerful that the dowser is thrown back from the stone when he touches it. Also pulses of energy have been measured travelling from stone to stone around a **stone circle** and long distances across country from one site to another. Such discoveries may hold clues to the meaning of **leys** – alignments of ancient sites.

Dowsers claim to be able to locate the energy pulses at and travelling between ancient sites by means of dowsing rods and pendulums. They are focusing their own innate sensitivity using these tools, and some dowsers use only their hands for dowsing. The problem with dowsing as a tool to investigate earth energies is that it has proved to be a highly subjective practice, shown by the fact that different dowsers prefer different methods and get different, often contradictory, results, so that it is inadvisable to trust any of them. Two or three decades ago, **leys** were being explained as energy lines, and dowsing was an important tool, but now ley researchers' attention has moved to **spirit lines** and the 'earth energy' theory has been discarded.

Dragons

St George is best known for his slaying of the dragon, but this event was not a one-off, and has been reenacted at different locations throughout Britain, and with assorted heroes and dragons. One of the places where St George is said to have slain the beast is on Dragon Hill, below **Uffington White Horse** in Oxfordshire (the white horse may possibly represent the dragon); another site for this event was a field close to Brinsop church in Herefordshire, where the slaying is depicted on an 11th-century carving in the church.

Author and antiquarian Harold Bayley, who in his book *The Lost Language of Symbolism* plays around with the basic meanings of words, interpreted 'George' as follows: '*Ge*, as in *geography*, meant *earth*, so that the true meaning of *George* may legitimately be surmised as *Ge urge*, the urger or stimulator of the Earth.' The dragon and the **serpent** have been used as symbols for rhythmic life, and they also have close links with **energy** and **fertility**: in the ancient Chinese art of **feng-shui**, the dragon lines of energy are believed to flow through the veins of the earth: could this be paralleled in Britain by earth currents or energies flowing along the alignments known as **leys**?

There are numerous dragon legends associated with natural landscape features and with **prehistoric sites** (for further details see our books *The Secret Country* and *The Enchanted Land*). English dragons were want to coil their long bodies around hills, as for example the Lambton Worm (dragons were often known as worms from their serpentine shape) which coiled around Worm Hill near Fatfield (Durham), and the dragon of Linton (Roxburgh) which had a den in Linton Hill, but sometimes coiled round another hill nearby, leaving spiral marks which still show where it lay. Dragons also appear in church carvings, sometimes being slain, and sometimes in a fertility connection, with foliage and fruit emerging from their mouths and tails. In all their manifestations in Britain, dragons are closely linked with life, power, energy.

Dragon Hill
See **Dragons; Uffington White Horse**

Dragon Project
Set up in the late 1970s, its purpose was to explore the idea that unusual energies are present at ancient sites, using both scientific and psychic approaches. Practical work began in the autumn of 1978, when a programme of monitoring the prehistoric sites at **Rollright** in Oxfordshire started. In 1980 round-the-clock monitoring was underway, involving ultrasonic detection, microwave monitoring, electric field detection, geiger monitoring, experimental infra-red photography, **dowsing** and clairvoyance. The research has continued for over 15 years, and measurable magnetic and radiation anomalies have been found at various sites, also anomalous light phenomena have been witnessed, and the significance of the findings is still being assessed. In the 1990s a **dream research** programme was undertaken. (*See also* **Earth lights; Energy.**)

Dream research
As part of the **Dragon Project**, a programme of dream research began in 1990, the aim of which was to study altered states of consciousness during sleep at selected places around Britain. The four sites chosen were **Carn Euny fogou**, Chun Quoit **dolmen** and Madron **holy well**, all in Cornwall, and Carn Ingli in Dyfed, Wales, a hilltop site with ancient stone walling and said to be the place where a Celtic saint experienced visions (*see* **Preseli Hills**). Volunteer dreamers slept at the sites, their dreams being logged by helpers and put into a computer so that the data can be analysed at the end of the experiment, which at the time of writing is expected to be some time during 1995.

Druids
Widely believed to be closely associated with prehistoric monuments such as **Stonehenge** and **Avebury**; in fact these sites were in use some 1500 years before the Druids were active. They were a powerful Celtic priesthood whose temples and sanctuaries were in sacred groves of oak **trees**. The very name 'Druid' is thought to relate to the Greek word for an oak tree, *drus*. They were powerful around the first century BC to the first century AD, and were wiped out by the Romans in AD 47, against whom they had led resistance,

and their last stand was on the island of Anglesey off the North Wales coast. A hoard of bronze and iron objects which was found in Llyn Cerrig Bach, an Anglesey lake, had Druid connections, but there is very little archaeological material that can be directly linked to them, and all the written descriptions come from Roman sources and are strongly biased against the Druids. Today's romantic ideas about the Druids are no more than modern fantasy, as too are the manifestations of so-called Druids today: they are a modern invention linked to the original Druids only by name. (*See also* **Celts**.)

Dunadd

An **Iron Age** fort was built on this isolated rock outcrop in western Scotland, and later it was probably the capital of the Scottish kingdom of Dalriada, established around AD 500 by colonists from Ireland. Dunadd may seem to be merely a rocky hill with a fine view over the surrounding flat countryside, but closer inspection reveals the relics which have made it such an intriguing place. On a flat slab of rock are carved an **Ogham** inscription, a boar, a **footprint**, and a rock basin. Judging from the function of similar carvings elsewhere, the last two were probably used in the rituals marking the **inauguration** of Dalriadan kings, the candidate placing his foot in the footprint to show that he would follow in the footsteps of his predecessors. The Ogham inscription has not yet been deciphered, but the boar is in the **Pictish** style and is thought to date from the time when the site was besieged and captured by Fergus, King of the Picts, in AD 736.

The visible remains on Dunadd are tantalizing; they hint of rituals long forgotten, yet vitally important to the people who practised them. There are many similar sites throughout Britain, that once were important places before being abandoned for some reason as the fortunes of communities ebbed and flowed. There may not be a lot to see, but such places, inhabited now only by wild birds and grazing sheep, can cause the imagination to fly back to an earlier age.

Location: 6.5 kilometres (4 miles) N of Lochgilphead, Argyll. OS ref: NR 837936.

E

Earth energies
See **Energy**

Earth-house
A Scottish name for a **fogou**.

Earth lights
People have always seen strange lights in the sky: today they are called **UFOs** and by many people interpreted as craft from sources outside Planet Earth. But there is strong evidence that a large proportion of UFO sightings are not of alien craft (indeed many people believe that *none* of the sightings are of alien craft). Some of the lights are thought to be caused by a natural phenomenon originating in the body of the earth. Earthquake activity is known to sometimes produce anomalous lights, and it is likely that these and other similar events are far more widespread than was ever imagined. These light effects were almost certainly also known to prehistoric man, and it could be that at least some of the stone monuments that our ancestors erected were sited with a view to utilizing natural **energy** in some way. Considerable research has been carried out into the earth light phenomenon by Paul Devereux, and his two books on the subject, *Earth Lights* and *Earth Lights Revelation*, provide very detailed information on his findings.

Earth Mother
There is some evidence that at one time, the earth was seen as a living body from which came all life, and to which all life returned. The survival and continuance of people, their crops and animals, was intimately bound up with the health of the Earth Mother, and people have always been careful to maintain the equilibrium of the life source. They may not always have been consciously aware of

why they performed certain practices, but we are still, albeit often unconsciously, instinctively aware of our close ties to the earth. Many agricultural practices and traditional **customs** over the centuries provide evidence for this.

People also saw the body of the Earth Mother in the landscape. Breast-shaped hills are an obvious example, sometimes given relevant names; and man-made hills were also seen as breasts. Wimble Toot ('teat'), a **tumulus** near Babcary in Somerset, lies on the breast of the Virgo figure in the controversial **Glastonbury zodiac**, a collection of gigantic figures said to be outlined by natural and man-made features in the Somerset landscape. Twin round **barrows** may also have been seen by their prehistoric builders as breasts and therefore as symbols of the Earth Mother. **Glastonbury Tor**, too, has been seen as a breast. On top is a church tower: is it only coincidence that hill and tower together strongly resemble a breast and nipple? Or were the church builders consciously locating the church where it could perform a dual pagan and Christian role?

Another feature of the body of the Earth Mother seen in the landscape is her womb, formed by mines and **caves**, **fogous** and **burial chambers**, **stone circles** and **holed stones**. Today we still see human heads (giants and saints, etc) in rock formations, and maybe at some deeper level we remember the days when we lived close to the Earth Mother, even on her body. (*See also* **Fertility; Mother goddess; Paganism**.)

Easter

The revival of life in spring-time is celebrated with eggs: in our culture they are most familiar as chocolate Easter eggs, but in the past people were rather more creative. The eggs were hard-boiled and coloured, egg-decorating being a highly skilled craft in many parts of the world. Then they were either eaten, or used in games such as egg-shackling (where the egg is used as a weapon to break others' eggs) and egg-rolling (where the eggs were rolled down a slope, being eaten after they cracked). Easter customs also involved the hare, which was the sacred animal of Eastre or Eostre, a Saxon goddess of spring and of the dawn, from whose name the festival is said to be derived. There was hare-hunting in some places, and at Hallaton in Leicestershire the Hare-Pie Scramble still takes place on Easter Monday.

Eildon Hills

These **fairy**-haunted hills in Scotland got their prominent shape when an evil spirit, at the command of the magician Michael Scot, split one large hill into three. There were tales of people visiting fairyland inside the hills – Thomas the Rhymer was taken there by the Fairy Queen and lived there for three years, though it seemed to him to be only three days. A horse trader called Canonbie Dick, who was taken into the hills, saw a large cavern where horses and knights lay sleeping – they were said to be King **Arthur's** men, awaiting the call to come to the country's aid. There are many other places throughout Britain where sleeping knights are said to be hidden. The old man who took Dick into the cavern gave him the choice of drawing a sword or blowing a horn, saying he would die if he chose wrongly. Dick chose the horn and blew a blast on it, whereupon all the knights and horses awoke. He grabbed the sword and heard a voice crying: 'Woe to the coward that ever he was born; Who did not draw the sword before he blew the horn.' Then he was whisked out of the hill in a whirlwind and was discovered lying on a bank by some shepherds, to whom he told his strange tale before he died.

Location: 1.5 kilometres (1 mile) S of Melrose, Roxburgh. OS ref: NT 5432.

Energy

Some people with unusual sensitivity say they are aware of energy pulses passing through the landscape, often moving from one **sacred site** to another. The method used to locate energy lines is **dowsing**, and it has been claimed to demonstrate all manner of weird and wonderful effects; but unfortunately it is very difficult to prove the objectivity of the dowsers' findings. The existence of energy currents within the earth was once a popular theory used to explain **leys**, but it has recently fallen out of favour, because of the difficulty of proving it, and because each researcher came up with different findings.

Nevertheless, the concept of earth energy should not be discarded completely. There are undoubtedly natural energies within the landscape, elusive and difficult to isolate, but that doesn't mean to say that our ancestors may not have found ways to make use of them. Some of the traditional **customs** practised so widely throughout Britain (and many of which still survive) may have been magical rites performed to raise energy and direct it to the desired goal, which was usually the **fertility** of crops, cattle, people, and the well-being of the land itself. When the rituals were performed at ancient sites, themselves already producing or channelling natural earth energies, then the energy available must have been considerably increased. There are many examples of customs being held at ancient sites, such as bonfires lit on **barrows**, the maypole erected above the **Cerne Abbas Giant**, and fairs held in earthworks. But it is as well to remember that there are no simple answers in our 20th-century search for earth energies. An account of the search for energies at ancient sites is given in *Places of Power* by Paul Devereux.

Excalibur

This was the magical sword given to King **Arthur** by the Lady of the Lake. Its scabbard prevented the wearer from losing blood. After Arthur's last battle, when he was near death, he made his knight Bedivere return it to the water. When he threw it in, a hand came up and grasped the sword, taking it down under the water. There are several locations suggested for this event, including Dozmary Pool on Bodmin Moor and Loe Pool in Mount's Bay, both in Cornwall, Llyn Llydaw in Snowdonia, Bosherston in Dyfed, and at Pomparles Bridge in **Glastonbury**.

Exhibitionist

This refers to sexual carvings of women and men displaying their genitals. The female carvings have been known as 'Sheela-na-gigs', though no one has convincingly explained this strange name. There are 40 or more such carvings in England, Scotland and Wales, and twice as many in Ireland. In Great Britain they are found carved on churches, the best example being at **Kilpeck** in Herefordshire. This carving (along with many other fine carvings on the exterior of the same church) is Romanesque or Norman, dating from around 1140. Male sexual carvings in churches are less common, but are occasionally found, as at Whittlesford in Cambridgeshire where a carving on the exterior of the church shows a naked woman and man, the latter with animal characteristics. There has been considerable debate as to the significance of these carvings, and it seems doubtful that they were intended to promote **fertility**, as the females are often hag-like and not at all attractive. It seems more likely that the carvings were intended to avert evil, in the same way that **phallus** carvings at Roman sites are thought to have done.

F

Fairies

The Little People have a strong association with the British countryside, and also with **prehistoric sites**, especially earthworks. The **Neolithic** round **barrow** known as Willy Howe in Humberside was a fairy dwelling, and one night a young man passing by heard sounds of merry-making. He saw a door in the mound, and inside were men and women eating and drinking. One of them brought out a cup for him, but he knew that if he drank from it he would become unconscious and be taken inside. So he poured away the contents and galloped off with the cup. When St Collen met the fairies who lived in **Glastonbury** Tor, he sprinkled them with holy water and they disappeared.

Entrances to Fairyland were to be found in all kinds of places, and the fairies would often come out to dance, this being one of their favourite pastimes. But any passing human who saw the fairies dancing, and felt compelled to join in, would be lost to his friends and family for many years, although the time he spent in Fairyland would to him seem only like an hour or two. Two fiddlers who went into Tom-na-Hurich Hill near Inverness to play for a fairy dance left the hill at dawn the next day: but when they looked in a mirror they saw two old men with long white beards, and someone told them that they had been gone for 100 years. They went into church, but crumbled into dust when the minister pronounced the blessing. Other fairy sites described in this book are **Dinas Bran, Eildon Hills,** and **Fairy Hill**.

Fairy Hill

There are many Fairy Hills in Britain, but there is a special one in Scotland which truly deserves its name. In the 17th century a Scottish clergyman, the Reverend Robert Kirk, wrote a study of the **fairies** called *The Secret Commonwealth of Elves, Fauns and Fairies*, after many years of collecting information from his parishioners.

In 1692 he died aged 48, while walking on a hill close to his home at Aberfoyle. A tradition grew up that he had not died, but had been kidnapped by the fairies, the hill being one of their dwelling places.

Kirk was allegedly buried in the old churchyard at Aberfoyle, but it was soon rumoured that the coffin was full of stones. It was also said that after his 'death' Kirk had appeared to a relative and told him that he was being held in fairyland but could be released. When the relative next saw Kirk's apparition – at the christening of Kirk's posthumous child – the relative was to throw a knife at him. This would break the spell because the fairies are powerless against iron. Sure enough, Kirk appeared at the ceremony, but the relative was so amazed he forgot to hurl the blade and Kirk's chance of release was lost for ever.

The hill where Kirk collapsed and 'died', and his grave, can still be visited. Fairy Hill or Doon Hill is an eerie place, even on a sunny day; its wooded slopes are littered with mossy boulders and it is easy to understand why this was believed to be a fairy haunt.
Location: At Aberfoyle, 13 kilometres (8 miles) SW of Callander, Perthshire. Waymarked paths encircle the hill; grave in old burial-ground at Kirkton S of village. Kirkton OS ref: NN 518005.

Female stones

There are a few instances of **standing stones** being shaped to represent the whole female body; or sometimes a natural stone has needed no extra shaping for it to be interpreted as a human body. Close to Grace's Well (Ffynnon Grassi) in Lady's Field beside Llyn Glasfryn, a lake at Llangybi (Gwynedd, North Wales), stands a stone that looks like a woman hurrying along. A local person remembered the stone being actually dressed in a bonnet and shawl, as if to reinforce its female identity. The field and neighbouring house were believed to be haunted by a tall female ghost, who was seen as recently as the last century. There was also a legend that the lake formed when the well overflowed after being accidentally left open – in other similar legends it was the female well guardian who forgot to close the well, and in view of the close proximity of the female stone, it seems likely that the same applied here, and that the stone represented the well guardian. With all the elements described, there are tantalizing hints of a lost tradition of potential significance.

Guernsey in the Channel Islands has two intriguing female

figures, both stones being roughly carved to represent the female body. This tradition goes back at least to **Neolithic** times: similar carved goddess figures have been found at prehistoric tombs. One of the Guernsey figures, known as *La Gran' mere du Catel*, stands in the churchyard of Catel church: until 1878 she lay unknown, buried a foot down. Was she the goddess of the sacred site which existed before the church was built there? The other is *La Gran'-mere du Chimquiere*, a granite stone at the gateway to the church of St Martin. Fruit and flowers used to be placed at her feet, in the hope of good fortune and **fertility**, especially on **May Day**. (*See also* **Offerings**.)

Diamond-shaped stones and **holed stones** have also been interpreted as female – *see* **Standing stones**.

Feng-shui

Literally 'wind and water', feng-shui is an ancient Chinese system of living in harmony with the landscape. Ch'i, an **energy** or life-force, flows through the ground like a stream along **dragon** lines, and its course can be changed by manipulating features on the earth. Good ch'i can be trapped, and brought to where it is needed, thus benefiting the **fertility** of man and the environment; while bad ch'i can be redirected away. The system is applied not only on a large scale, to landscapes with mountains and rivers, but also on a much smaller scale in the positioning of windows and doorways within a house. The principles of feng-shui are not solely relevant to China, but are equally applicable in the West. (*See also* **Leys**.)

Fertility

One of the major preoccupations of humankind is with fertility, and always has been; after all, without fertility, Man as a species would die out. It is not only the fertility of the people which is vital, but also the fertility of the earth, of crops and animals, for without them our existence would be hard indeed. Our predecessors evolved and successfully practised ways of maintaining fertility in man/woman, beast and land, and these have come down to us in the form of customs and rituals now performed without knowledge of their original purpose. We published a study of early fertility practices in Britain in our now out-of-print book *Earth Rites: Fertility Practices in Pre-Industrial Britain*, and some of the ideas we included were: natural landscape features being interpreted as parts of the **Earth Mother's** body (hills and tumuli as breasts, for example), and prehistoric structures seen as her womb (e.g. **Stonehenge, burial chambers**); **standing stones** being seen as phallic symbols or female symbols depending on their shape (*see* **Avebury; Phallus**); rituals connected with betrothal and marriage being performed at certain stones, for example **holed stones**; other stones being resorted to in order to ensure fertility or cure barrenness; sexual themes being carved in Christian churches (*see* **Carvings in churches; Exhibitionist**); the veneration of water (*see* **Holy wells**) and **trees**; and surviving traditional **customs** of all kinds that may have had their origins in early fertility practices. Once you start looking, you can see sex and fertility everywhere, but without them the human race would have disappeared long ago!

Fire ceremonies

Throughout the year, on the appropriate date, ceremonial bonfires were lit, and these fire festivals were all concerned with various aspects of **fertility**. There were eight of these significant dates, and they fall into two groups of four. Four of them were related to the movements of the moon and four to the sun. The lunar fire festivals were **Samhain** (1 November), Imbolc/Oimelc (1 February), Beltane (1 May) and Lugnasad/Lammas (1 August); and those which were derived from the sun's apparent movement were on or near 22 December (the Winter Solstice), 21 March (the Spring Equinox), 22 June (the Summer Solstice) and 23 September (the Autumn Equinox). Thus throughout the year there was a balanced interlocking of the feminine – lunar – **earth mother** forces with those of the masculine – solar – sky father. The painstaking surveys of Professor Thom have shown that many **stone circles** and alignments, some as old as 4,000 years, are positioned to mark some of these sacred dates.

We have space here to mention only a few of the many fire ceremonies that have been practised in Britain, like the flaming cartwheels, bound with straw and pitch, which were sent bowling down hillsides in order to quicken the powers of the dying sun, and the act of jumping over a blazing bonfire to gain **fertility** and good fortune, and the scattering of ashes over the crops to help them grow, and carrying burning barrels round the town early in January to bring good luck in the new year, and so on . . . Today only a few of these fire customs survive, notably the bonfires lit throughout the country on 5 November, ostensibly to commemorate the Gunpowder Plot and the capture of Guy Fawkes, whose effigy is often still burnt. Originally the early November fires were lit to mark Samhain, the start of the Celtic year: the fire would challenge the cold and darkness of the coming winter. The effigy burned on the fire probably symbolized all the malevolent forces with which the community had had to contend in the preceding year.

Fogou

Called souterrains or earth-houses in Scotland, fogous are **underground passages** or chambers made of stone that were sometimes constructed in **Iron Age** settlements. A good example can be seen at **Carn Euny settlement** in Cornwall. They are conventionally thought to have been used as food stores and refuges in time of war, but it is possible that they also had a religious or ritual function. In the early 1990s the fogou at Carn Euny was used as one of the locations for the **Dragon Project's dream research** programme: a volunteer would sleep in the fogou and would record his or her dreams, assisted by a helper, the aim being to discover if such a place could affect dream content.

Folklore

Natural and man-made features have all attracted folklore, especially tales about how the place came into being, and these usually involved the **Devil** or **giants**. Such tales are never originated by any one person: they just seem to spring up from nowhere, and are passed on from person to person down the generations, often being elaborated in the telling. They may have their origins many hundreds of years ago, some perhaps even in prehistoric times, but few written records exist whereby their development can be traced. The impulse to invent or share stories continues today, but modern folklore takes the form of 'urban legends' with such stories as the deadly spider in the house-plant or in the beehive hairdo, the granny on the roof-rack, and the hairy-armed 'female' hitchhiker.

The entries in this book which are concerned with folklore include: **Cock-crow stones; Countless Stones; Devil; Devil's Arrows; Dinas Bran; Dragons; Eildon Hills; Fairies; Footprints; Giants; Glastonbury; Mermaids; Moving stones; Petrifaction; Rollright Stones; St Govan's Chapel; Treasure; Underground passages; Wishing stones and wells; The Wrekin.**

Footprints

In folklore there are many tales telling how saints, the **Devil**, the Virgin Mary, King **Arthur** and others have left visible traces of themselves on the British landscape. Footprints are the most common, such as St Columba's near the **holy well** and ancient chapel at Keil in Argyll, Owain Glyndwr's at Corwen in Clwyd, and the Devil's at several places including Llanymynech Hill in Shropshire; but fingerprints are also seen (like St Tydecho's at his holy well in the mountains of Gwynedd), and knee marks, and rock hollows showing where the Devil sat. Animals have also left their marks on rocks, usually horses' hoofprints: St George's horse left its prints on a stone at St George in Clwyd, while the marks of King Arthur's horse are visible in several places. Many other fascinating examples are described in our book *The Enchanted Land*.

G

Gawain

Sir Gawain was one of King **Arthur's** knights. In the 14th-century poem *Sir Gawain and the Green Knight*, he cut off the Green Knight's head, but the knight picked it up again and told Gawain to meet him on New Year's Morning for the blow to be returned. The Green Knight may have links with the **green man**. Gawain is said to have become a hermit following Arthur's death, possibly living (and eventually dying) on the Pembrokeshire coast, at the site of **St Govan's Chapel**. (St Govan is a very obscure saint, and Govan and Gawain may be the same.) His tomb is said to be beneath the altar in the small chapel; his skull is said to be at Dover Castle (Kent).

Geomancy

Literally 'earth divination', geomancy encompasses all the ways in which people lived in harmony with the landscape in past ages. Much of the knowledge they possessed has been lost, or survives only as **folklore**. (*See also* **Energy; Feng-shui**.) The scope of geomancy is clearly shown in Nigel Pennick's book *The Ancient Science of Geomancy*.

Giants

If folklore is to be believed, giants once peopled the earth, and were also responsible for many of Britain's notable landscape features. There are still two giants to be seen: the **Cerne Abbas Giant** in Dorset, and the **Long Man of Wilmington** in East Sussex – both **hill figures** cut into the landscape many hundreds of years ago. (*See also* **Gogmagog giants**.) As for legendary giants, they formed numerous hills such as **The Wrekin** in Shropshire, and rocky outcrops like St Michael's Mount in Cornwall. That was once a forest stronghold, built by the giant Cormoran and his wife Cormelian from white granite which they fetched from some distance away, carrying it back in their aprons. One day when

Cormoran was sleeping, Cormelian decided to bring some green-stone from a much nearer source, but he woke up and kicked her, so that her apron-string broke and the rock fell to the ground. Now St Michael's Mount is offshore and surrounded by water, and the greenstone rock, known as Chapel Rock, can be seen beside the causeway leading across the bay to the Mount. Many other examples of landscape features formed by giants can be found in our book *The Enchanted Land*.

Ghosts

Prehistoric sites can be eerie places, out on the moorland in swirling mists, and it would be easy to people them with ghosts. Perhaps some of the ghosts seen at such places are only imaginary, but it is also possible that echoes of past events do linger, to be sensed and somehow brought into vision at a later date by someone visiting a site and tuning in to the right wavelength. This was probably what happened at a Northumberland **Iron Age hill-fort** close to a hut where a man was staying in the 1970s. He awoke one night to find a girl standing over him. She wore a plaid shawl fastened with a Celtic brooch, and looked very sad. She faded away as he looked at her. At other times she appeared to two other men: all three witnesses were, strangely, named Ray. She always appeared in the same spot, only 54 metres (60 yards) from the hill-fort's gateway. Further south, in Dorset, an archaeologist saw the ghost of a bare-legged horseman wearing a long grey cloak and riding without bridle or stirrups. He galloped alongside the witness's car before disappearing by a prehistoric round **barrow**. He was also seen on another occasion by a shepherd, who asked him for a light, not realizing the solid-looking figure was a ghost. At **Avebury**, figures have been seen among the **standing stones**. Phantom **black dogs** have sometimes been seen close to barrows, acting as **treasure** guardians perhaps. Some **holy wells** are also haunted, but as most well ghosts are female, they are likely to be distorted memories of pagan water goddesses.

Glastonbury

During the last 30 years Glastonbury has become a New Age 'Mecca', drawing in visitors from all over the world, eager to savour its mystical atmosphere. The historical figure most associated with Glastonbury is King **Arthur**, who may or may not have been a real person – no one knows for certain. His name was first linked to Glastonbury in the early 12th century by Caradoc of Llancarfan, and at the end of that century his grave was discovered in the abbey. Gerald of Wales wrote (in Latin) about the 1191 excavation, which he may have witnessed, saying that the bodies of a man and a woman, thought to be Arthur and his wife Guinevere, were found in a hollow oak coffin set between two stone pyramids. A tress of yellow hair was also found, but when it was seized by a monk it fell into dust. Arthur's bones were huge, and ten wounds were visible, all scarred over except one, larger than the rest, which had presumably caused his death. A lead cross was also found, bearing the words 'Here lies buried the renowned King Arthur, with Guinevere his second wife, in the isle of Avalon'.

There is controversy over whether this really was King Arthur's grave, or whether it was a hoax concocted by the monks in order to obtain money to rebuild the abbey which had been destroyed by fire in 1184, only a few years before the body was discovered. A shrine to Arthur was set up, and the site has attracted visitors ever since. Today in the abbey ruins the original location of the grave is marked, and also one of the sites where the remains were later placed. There are other interesting features in the abbey ruins, including the Lady Chapel, but Arthur's Grave clearly takes precedence in a book on mysteries.

Joseph of Arimathea, a secret disciple of Jesus who had begged his body from Pilate and buried it in a new rock-cut tomb, is another figure with strong (if legendary) Glastonbury connections. He was said to be the leader of the missionaries who came to Glastonbury in AD 63 and built the first church there. Its location was where the Lady Chapel (also St Mary Chapel or St Joseph Chapel) now stands. When on his arrival St Joseph rested on Wirral (Wearyall) Hill, he stuck his staff into the ground and it burst into flower. Descendants of this thorn **tree** flower at Christmas – there is still a specimen in the abbey grounds. Joseph was also said to have carried the **Holy Grail** with him to England – the Grail was the cup that received Christ's blood at Calvary – and it was hidden in **Chalice Well** at the foot of the Tor, which is why the water appears reddish in colour. St Joseph's grave was believed to be at Glastonbury, but it was never found.

The other major feature of the Glastonbury landscape is the Tor, a prominent, steep-sided hill overlooking the town which has clearly been an important site for many centuries, as is shown by the church tower which still stands on the summit. The terraces on the slopes also indicate man's early use of the hill: but are they simply cultivation platforms, or evidence of a huge three-dimensional **maze**, as suggested by Geoffrey Russell in the 1960s? If the latter, the maze-like processional paths may have been built as early as two or three thousand years BC, meaning that the Tor has been a religious focus for at least 4,000 years.

An archaeological excavation in the 1960s unearthed flints from c.10,000-1000 BC and a **Neolithic** polished axe, some Roman pottery and tile, and traces of a dark-age settlement with postholes and graves, metal-working hearths and a bronze head-mask. The Tor may have been one of the earliest monastic sites in Britain (late 5th or early 6th century). Early in the 7th century an Anglo-Saxon monastery was built, then a stone church in the 12th or 13th century, which fell in an earthquake in 1275. A second church was built in 1323-34: both churches were dedicated to St Michael the Archangel, as churches on high places often were. The tower of this church still survives, and some carvings can be seen – possibly St Bridget milking a cow (*see* **Bride**), and St Michael holding scales. The hilltop church may have been the focal point of a cult of St Michael. At the Dissolution of the Monasteries (which began in 1536), the last Abbot of Glastonbury and two monks were hanged on the Tor.

These are the known facts of the Tor's history. It has several other claims to fame, including the tale of the 6th-century St Collen, who is said to have met the king of the **fairies**, Gwyn ap Nudd, who lived in the fairy land of Annwn. Messengers from Gwyn ap Nudd summoned Collen three times, but he was fearful, and only went to the meeting on top of the Tor because they threatened him. He took a vial of holy water for protection, and on the hilltop saw a fine castle with young men and women and horses all around. Gwyn ap Nudd, who was sitting on a golden chair, invited him to eat, but he refused, and sprinkled his holy water around, at which everything disappeared and he was alone on the silent hill.

The Tor also has an Arthurian connection, according to Caradoc's Life of Gildas. Arthur's wife Guinevere was kidnapped by Melwas, King of Somerset, and taken to his fortress, probably on the Tor. Arthur arrived with an army to rescue her, but a treaty was arranged before any battle was fought. The Tor also lies inside the **Glastonbury Zodiac**, a circle 16 kilometres (10 miles) across taking in many landscape features which outline the zodiac figures. The Tor lies in the head of a phoenix which represents

Aquarius. The Glastonbury **ley** in Paul Devereux and Ian Thomson's *The Ley Hunter's Companion* passes through the Tor (although in his later revision, *The New Ley Hunter's Guide*, Devereux has discarded this ley). The Tor is also on the **St Michael Line**, a long-distance ley running from Cornwall to Norfolk. In addition, strange lights have been seen over the hill (*see* **Earth lights**), adding to the air of mystery which surrounds it. The Tor is a classic **holy hill**.

Location: Glastonbury is 17.5 kilometres (11 miles) E of Bridgwater, Somerset, and the Tor is just E of the town. Tor OS ref: ST 512386.

Glastonbury Zodiac

In 1925, inspired by reading *The High History of the Holy Grail*, Katherine Maltwood began to plot 'Merlin's Round Table of the Grail in the Valleys of Avalon', and found that 'enormous effigies resembling Zodiacal creatures arranged in a circle' could be located in the Glastonbury countryside, their outlines formed by landscape features both natural and manmade. Sixteen kilometres (10 miles) across, the zodiac includes a lion, virgin, scorpion, centaur, goat, phoenix, fishes, ram, bull, giant, hare, birds, dog. Glastonbury itself falls within the phoenix (which represents the Aquarius figure), and in her book *A Guide to Glastonbury's Temple of the Stars*, Katherine Maltwood describes the imaginary view from the Tor:

> The Lion is out of sight from the Tor, for he is lying on the slope of the hills opposite Somerton, in order to get the full glare of the south sun in his months of July and August. Towards the East, Virgo reclines, outlined by the Cary river; she looks like an old witch with a broomstick, dressed in high bonnet, and flowing garment sufficiently voluminous to hide the host of babies she has produced from its folds. Further East, with the right claws lying along the River Brue, sprawls the gigantic Scorpion, waiting to catch the unwary. Then next in the ring comes Hercules like a Centaur, for he has been thrown on to the shoulders of his kneeling horse, south west of the Pennard Hills. North of this horse of the sun, the Goat lies, showing off his wonderful horn, Ponter's Ball . . . [Ponter's Ball is an ancient earthwork.]

Far-fetched or inspired? Although historians and archaeologists are sceptical as to the objective reality of terrestrial zodiacs, other researchers have found zodiacs elsewhere in Britain, for example Holderness, Nuthampstead, Kingston, and Pumpsaint in South Wales – over 60 have been claimed since the 1960s.

Goddess
See **Bride; Coventina's Well; Earth Mother; Female stones; Mother goddess**.

Gogmagog Giants
Hill figures by this name used to exist in Cambridgeshire and Devon. The **Iron Age hillfort** Wandlebury Camp is the location for the Cambridgeshire giants, whose outline was rediscovered by archaeologist T.C. Lethbridge in 1954 using a 'sounding-bar' to test the ground. During previous centuries there were written references to the giants, but by this century they had become totally overgrown and lost. What Lethbridge in fact found was a female giantess, whom he identified with the Celtic horse-goddess Epona, together with a Celtic sword-carrying warrior and a sun-god with flying cloak. The giantess **Earth Mother** was Magog, the sun-god was Gog, or so the theory ran.

In Devon, the Gogmagog Giants were cut on a steep slope overlooking Plymouth Sound, but again are no longer visible. According to legend, as written by Geoffrey of Monmouth, 12th-century chronicler, in his *History of the Kings of Britain*, the giant Goemagot wrestled with a Trojan, Prince Corineus, and was thrown down into the sea by him, the place where he fell being afterwards known as Goemagot's Leap. (*See also* **Giants**.)

Gop Cairn
This impressive but little-known **cairn** rivals **Silbury Hill**, which is the only larger **barrow** (if that is what either or both of them are) in Britain. It stands about 12 metres (40 feet) high, and a shaft dug in from the top just over 100 years ago located only a few horse and ox bones, so there is no certainty that it contains a **burial chamber**; though bodies were found in a cave lower down the Hill of the Arrows on which the cairn stands. In folklore the cairn was claimed to be Queen Boudicca's (Boadicea) burial place, or alternatively a Roman general was buried there. In 1938 a local man saw the ghost of a Roman general on a white horse on the hill, and not

far away he saw a field full of Roman soldiers.
Location: 2.5 kilometres (1½ miles) SE of Prestatyn, Clwyd, reached
by footpath from Trelawnyd. OS ref: SJ 087802.

Grail
See **Holy Grail**

Green man
The green man may be an example of a pagan symbol found in a
Christian church (*see* **Paganism**). Another way of describing the
green man is as a 'foliate head', and this image has been traced
back to Roman art of the first century AD. The theme spread to
Britain soon after the Norman Conquest, but the majority of carvings seem to date from the 13th, 14th and 15th centuries. Foliage
and heads (usually human, sometimes animal) are the main
features, but there are variations in design. A human face may
peep out through foliage; a human face is formed of foliage,
usually shown by the hair and edges of the face being carved as
foliage; a face sprouts foliage from the mouth (most often) or sometimes the nose, eyes, or ears. Green men may be found carved on
roof bosses, corbels, capitals, fonts, tympana, tombs (all stone), and
screens, bench-ends and misericords (all wood) – in fact, wherever
there are carvings in churches. The carvings vary as much as the
modern interpretations of them, but most popular is that they
represent the **Jack-in-the-Green** figure of the May celebrations.
The similarity between the foliage framework hiding a man who
peeped out through a small hole, and the carved face peering out
through leaves, was first noticed by Lady Raglan, who also seems
to have been the first person to identify the foliate head theme in
church carving. Since the Jack in the Green seems to have symbolized the renewal of life in spring, the link with the church carving is
compelling, especially with the most often seen variation, the face
with foliage sprouting from it.

Variants of this theme suggest that the carvings depict tree-
spirits or demons (the faces are often ugly or evil), or illustrate the
continuance of **tree**-worship. Followers of the 'Old Religion' or
witchcraft have seen the foliate head as the 'Old God', but just as
plausible (or implausible, depending on one's beliefs) is the idea
that these heads, and the other heads without foliage that are seen
so often in churches, represent a survival of the **head-cult** which
was so important in the Celtic culture. In support of the idea that

the carvings represent gods of some kind, it is interesting to note that there are carvings of Roman deities emerging from leaves; for example on the capital of the 3rd-century AD Jupiter column from Corinium (Cirencester) in Gloucestershire, which depicts two male and two female deities.

Although some of the faces are devilish and evil, others seem friendly and beneficent. It seems possible that at least some of these carvings incorporated a **fertility** theme, and were meant to depict the natural cycle of death and rebirth: signifying that at death bodies decompose to earth, from which springs the next generation.

H

Hallowe'en
See **Samhain**

Head-cult
It is debatable whether there ever was a head-cult as such, but there can be no doubt that the human head was an important symbol in earlier times, being seen as the place where the spirit resided. It was often associated with the **phallus**, and so was also connected with sexual themes and **fertility**. The **Celts** collected the heads of their victims and displayed them on stakes, believing them to be a source of fertility. They also combined the phallus and the head, carving heads on the glans of phallic stones, and so any stones thus decorated must have symbolized a powerful potency.

The Celtic cult of the head was also associated with **water** worship. There is varied evidence for this, such as the discovery of human skulls in wells and pools, and tales in which people were decapitated and their heads thrown into wells. Some wells miraculously appeared where a severed head fell, such as **St Winefride's Well** at Holywell in Clwyd. Winefride did not respond to the amorous advances of Prince Caradoc, who promptly beheaded her. Where her head fell, water gushed from the earth; and Winefride herself was saved when her uncle St Beuno picked up her head and placed it back on her shoulders. At other **holy wells** it was the custom to drink the water from a human skull.

Human heads are also abundant in Christian churches, where they have been used as decoration inside and out. Whether they were merely intended as decoration, or had a deeper significance, is uncertain, though some of them probably did. The belief that the head was the receptacle for the spirit probably prompted the use of heads as decoration in religious buildings; but a different meaning may have been intended by the strange foliate heads or **green men**, who have leaves sprouting from their faces.

Healing

Many ancient stones were visited for healing purposes, especially **holed stones**. The most famous example is probably the **Men-an-Tol** in Cornwall: prevention and cure of a variety of illnesses of a rheumatic nature could be obtained by crawling through the hole in the central stone, or, if a sick child was brought for a cure, by passing it through the hole, in addition to following certain rituals. These included passing a scrofulous child naked through the hole three times and then dragging it along the grass three times in an easterly direction. Adults suffering from ague had to crawl through the hole nine times against the sun. The Tolmen, a holed stone in the North Teign River on Dartmoor (Devon), would protect against rheumatic complaints, but it was necessary to climb on to it and drop through to the stone slab below, not a particularly easy procedure. Similarly the cure obtainable at the Drake Stone in the Harbottle Hills of Northumberland was not easy to achieve: the stone is 9 metres (30 feet) high, and sick children had to be passed over the top of it. When a holed stone in Brahan Wood, Dingwall (Ross & Cromarty) was used to heal sick children, cake-divination was also practised, even into the early years of this century. The woman of the family would bake cakes at the holed stone and then leave them on top of it. If they had vanished next morning, it was believed that the patient would recover, but if they were still there, it was a bad sign.

Small portable holed stones were also used for healing purposes: in Suffolk it was believed that a holed stone tied to the bed-head would prevent nightmares. In Scotland, the stitch-stones of Ross & Cromarty could be used to cure all kinds of ailments from sciatica to pleurisy. The last person to use them would pass them on when needed by someone else. Some healing stones were dipped in water, and the water was then drunk by the sick person (or animal). The Clach Dearg or Red Stone belonged to the Campbells of Ardvorlich (Perth) and the water in which it had been dipped was used to cure distemper.

The other great healer was the water of **holy wells**. Most holy wells in Britain (and there were thousands) were believed to be able to cure some ailment, and some were said to cure anything. Others were named from the illness they specialized in: Eye Well, Cholic Well, Gout Well, for instance. As at stones, certain rituals often had to be performed. Sometimes it was enough simply to take a drink of the water; but at other wells total or partial immersion was necessary, and at such wells a bathing pool would be provided. A special incantation might have to be recited, or the patient would have to walk round the well a certain number of times, or sleep overnight on the nearby saint's chair (a chair-shaped stone). Sometimes the ritual involved a nearby **tree**, with the patient leaving a piece of rag tied to a twig, perhaps symbolizing the leaving behind of the illness: as the rag rotted, so too would the illness fade away. Sometimes offerings such as pins (often bent) or pebbles would be dropped into the water. There is no doubt that some holy well cures did work; and some wells are still visited by people seeking a cure, for example **St Winefride's Well** in Clwyd. Much more information on healing wells can be found in our book *Sacred Waters*; while more examples of healing stones can be found in *The Secret Country*. (See also the holy well magazine *Source*.)

Henge
A circular prehistoric monument dating from **Neolithic** times: a bank with a ditch outside enclosed an area from 45 to 180 metres (150–2000 feet) across, and some henges contained burials, pits, or stone circles (as at **Stonehenge** and **Avebury**). They are believed to have been places where rituals were performed.

Herefordshire Beacon hillfort
Set high in the Malvern Hills, the banks and ditches of this **Iron Age** fort are still impressive, as they snake along the hilltop, roughly following the contour line, and enclosing an area of 13 hectares (32 acres). On a clear day the views are magnificent.
Location: 5 kilometres (3 miles) SW of Great Malvern, Hereford & Worcester; access from large car park opposite British Camp Hotel. OS ref: SO 760400.

Hill o' Many Stanes
Although visually unimpressive, this is a site of major importance for the study of prehistoric **astronomy**. In a remote location in northern Scotland, around 200 small stones are arranged in 22 apparently parallel rows, in fact slightly fan-shaped. Professor Alexander Thom, who surveyed many **prehistoric sites** and wrote several detailed books on his findings, interpreted the grid of stones as an early computer, used to plot the positions of the moon about 4,000 years ago.
Location: 14.5 kilometres (9 miles) SW of Wick, Caithness. OS ref: ND 295384.

Hill Figures

From time to time men have been moved to carve giant figures on chalk hillsides in southern England: the earliest dates back as far as the Bronze Age – the **Uffington White Horse** in Oxfordshire. There are several other white horses, much younger though still maybe originating over a hundred years ago; but the two other ancient hill figures, both rather mysterious, are the **Cerne Abbas Giant** in Dorset and the **Long Man of Wilmington** in East Sussex. There are around 50 hill figures in England all told, though some have been lost through neglect, such as the very strange **Gogmagog Giants** at Wandlebury Camp in Cambridgeshire and at Plymouth in Devon, and a red horse (red because of the soil colour) at Tysoe in Warwickshire.

Hillfort

The earliest hillforts in Britain date from the late **Bronze Age** and early **Iron Age**, around 3000 years ago. Banks and ditches were dug to fortify a hilltop, so that the people could live inside and be safe from attacks by their enemies. Other types of forts were built if there were no hilltops: plateau forts were built on low-lying ground, promontory forts and cliff-castles used coastal peninsulas and headlands, defences being built at the 'neck' where the headland joined the mainland. Traces of settlements have been discovered inside hillforts, and sometimes a large-scale excavation has been able to piece together many details of the occupants' lifestyle. Over 2,500 hillforts survive in Britain and one of the most impressive is **Maiden Castle** in Dorset. (*See also* **Herefordshire Beacon hillfort**.)

Hobby horse

See **Abbots Bromley Horn Dance; Horse**

Holed stones

Holed stones may have symbolized the female principle: at some **prehistoric sites** female holed stones were close to male phallic stones, as for example at the **Men-an-Tol**. This may explain why they were often visited and rituals performed with the expectation of ensuring **fertility** or curing barrenness. Earlier in the marital sequence, couples visited certain holed stones to seal their betrothal, as at Tresco in the Scilly Isles, where in the old abbey gardens there was a stone with two holes. Engaged couples would grasp each other's hands through the holes and so 'plight their troth'. Another holed stone used in this way was the Stone of Odin on Orkney mainland, while at Lairg in Sutherland there was a 'Plightin' Stane' built into the church wall.

In some places actual marriages were performed at holed stones, for example at Kirk Braddan on the Isle of Man. During the wedding ceremony, the couple would clasp hands through the hole in one of the holed stones in the churchyard. This may have symbolized entry into a new life, and may have a link with the holed stones at some prehistoric **burial chambers** (*see, for example,* **Trethevy Quoit**). It has been suggested that these holes were to allow the bones of the dead to be passed through, signifying the door into another world, or moving from one life to another, as is the case with both marriage and death. This idea of passage from one form of existence to another is also seen at holed stones that were used to cure illnesses, such as the Men-an-Tol mentioned earlier. Sick people would crawl through the hole, or sick children were passed through, in hopes of a future life without the unwanted affliction. (*See also* **Healing**.)

Holy Grail

The cup or chalice used by Christ at the Last Supper: it was saved by Joseph of Arimathea, along with some of Christ's blood at the time of the Crucifixion. Joseph brought it to England, where it was lost. It was said to vanish when anyone who was not wholly pure approached it, and the Knights of the **Round Table** embarked on a quest for it. There are several medieval stories about the Grail, including the *Roman de Perceval*, *Perlesvaus (The High History of the Holy Grail)*, and *Parzival*, and it has remained a subject of burning interest. There are also non-Christian aspects to the story: in Celtic tales it was a magic cauldron offering endless food, or rebirth for dead warriors, or inspiration. The Holy Grail has been interpreted in many different ways through the centuries. There are places in Britain where it is said to be hidden, the best known of these being **Chalice Well** at Glastonbury, and another being the hill **Dinas Bran** in Wales.

Holy hill

Some alignments or **leys** appear to focus on special hills which can be thought of as sacred or holy hills. For example, a ley at Winchester in Hampshire focuses on St Catherine's Hill, and leys at the three **hill figures** of **Uffington White Horse, Cerne Abbas Giant** and **The Long Man of Wilmington** all pass through the notable hills on which the figures were placed; and all these hills have other prehistoric features on them. More details of these sites and their leys can be found in Paul Devereux's *The New Ley Hunter's Guide.* (*See also* **Glastonbury** for details of the holy hill of Glastonbury Tor.)

Holy Island
See **Lindisfarne; Isles, sacred**

Holy well
Natural **water** supplies in the form of rivers, streams, pools, springs and wells have seemingly always been venerated, which is not surprising in view of the vital role water plays in man's existence. By the time the Celtic culture was established in Britain, which happened several hundred years BC, water worship was an important and complex aspect of religious practice. **Bronze Age** people and the early **Celts** saw wells as entrances to the underworld and cut ritual wells, pits and shafts deep into the earth. One near **Stonehenge** is about 33 metres (110 feet) deep. Objects presumably intended as offerings to the gods – pottery, bones, coins, pebbles – were thrown into these shafts.

The Celts believed that water conveyed **fertility**, and the Celtic **mother goddesses**, also much involved with fertility, became linked to sacred water sources. One well where this happened was at the Roman fort of Brocolitia (Carrawburgh) on Hadrian's Wall. The well was dedicated to Coventina, who was probably a local goddess adopted by the Romans. Over 14,000 coins, together with other offerings like glass, pottery, and bronze figures, dating from pre-Roman times up to the 4th century AD, were found in the well, as were 24 altars, possibly hidden there when the shrine was attacked. A well-preserved stone tablet shows Coventina lying on water plants and an urn, and holding another plant. (*See* **Coventina's Well**.)

Sacred waters did not lose their importance when Christianity became the dominant religion in Britain. Many holy wells were dedicated to Christian saints, and often a story involving the saint was told to explain how the well came into existence. For example, wells sometimes sprang up where saints' bodies were briefly laid during their last journey. Two wells mark the death of Ethelbert,

King of East Anglia, who was murdered by order of King Offa of Mercia while Ethelbert was his guest, as a suitor of Offa's daughter. Miracles were soon reported at Ethelbert's grave at Marden in Herefordshire, and when the body was removed to Hereford a spring began to flow in the empty grave. At the place in Hereford where the body briefly lay, St Ethelbert's Well began to flow, and King Offa, regretting the murder, had a shrine erected to Ethelbert's memory in 795, on the site of which now stands Hereford Cathedral, of which Ethelbert is the patron saint. (St Ethelbert's Well at Marden can still be seen, inside the church; and the site of St Ethelbert's Well at Hereford is near the entrance to Castle Green.)

People visited holy wells to seek cures for a variety of illnesses, often leaving offerings in the water, and most wells were famed for their ability to cure, some curing only specific diseases, others curing many different ailments. Some wells were claimed to have the power of divination or prophecy; some were used to curse one's enemies. Some holy wells are still visited by people seeking cures, for example **St Winefride's Well** at Holywell. (*See also* **Healing**.) In some parts of the country **well-dressing** is a popular custom, the local wells being decorated with elaborate pictures made of flowers, leaves, seeds and other natural objects.

The well has been interpreted as a secret entrance into the body of the **Earth Mother** or even as her womb, and before saints took over the holy wells it is likely that pagan goddesses were worshipped there. A long-standing belief in the life-giving powers of water developed into the belief that wells were a source of fertility, and women used to visit them to cure barrenness. The Well of Fertility on the Isle of Skye was reputed to make barren cattle fertile, and was also secretly visited by barren women. Bride's Well near Corgarff in Grampian was visited by a bride on the evening before her marriage. She would bathe her feet and upper body in well water, to ensure that she would have children, and she placed a little bread and cheese in the well so that they would never go hungry. There are many other examples of fertility wells in Britain, one doubly powerful one being at Burwell in Cambridgeshire which would ensure male twins for women who drank the water.

Holy wells also had close links with special **trees**, and the two are often found together. This may be because the well represents the female and the tree represents the male. This does not necessarily refer to the phallic shape of the tree, since not all trees have this shape. Many are rounded, and others, like thorn trees, are relatively small. The contrast lies rather in the receptive, inward-looking nature of the well and the vital, outward-growing nature of the tree. People visiting holy wells for cures would often leave behind a piece of rag tied to the nearby rag-bush, and some were used as places to hang votive offerings, such as the ash at the Well of the Ash-tree on the Isle of Man.

Further information on holy wells can be found in our earlier book *Sacred Waters* (now out of print); see also the holy wells journal *Source*.

Horned god

The horn is a symbol of strength, power and virility, and the Celtic horned or antlered gods were widely worshipped. They also had a powerful **fertility** symbolism, especially for crops and vegetation. The best known pagan horned god is Cernunnos, the stag god, the lord of the animals – his cult was so powerful that it was banned by the early Christians. He was used as a symbol of the anti-Christ on Christian crosses, and the **Devil** was sometimes depicted with horns, so that a positive figure of power and virility was turned into a negative figure symbolizing lust.

Other horned deities, with the same attributes as Cernunnos, include Herne the Hunter, a pagan stag-god said to haunt Windsor Forest; and horned gods are surely represented in some ancient traditional customs with men wearing antlers, especially the **Abbots Bromley Horn Dance**.

Horse

Animal disguises featured in traditional **customs**, and the most frequent animal disguise recorded in Britain is the horse. A man would dress in a horse costume, and often the party would go from house to house singing songs. Customs like this include the Hooden Horse of Kent and the Mari Llwyd of South Wales. Another manifestation is the 'Obby 'Oss (hobby horse) of Padstow in Cornwall, who appears at a **May Day** celebration which is still very active, in contrast to many of the other horse customs. The 'Oss is made of a circular frame about 2 metres (6 feet) across which is covered with black oilskin and is carried on a man's shoulders. A skirt of black oilskin drapes down from the circumference of the frame. At the front is a small carved horse's head and at the rear is a tail of horse hair. The operator, whose head projects from a hole in the centre of the 'Oss, wears a strangely painted mask with a tall pointed hat. In front of the 'Oss goes the Dancer or Teaser who waves a 'club' which is a small shield-shaped bat with a handle. His or her job is to dance and twist about in front of the 'Oss to encourage it to do likewise. The 'Oss swirls, prances and leaps, barely missing the packed onlookers who line the narrow streets of this small fishing town. As he dances, the 'Oss is accompanied by the mayers dressed all in white, dancing to the haunting tune played by the accompanying musicians. Sometimes the 'Oss jumps towards a young woman and covers her with his skirt. This is taken to mean that she will soon have a husband or a baby, and is part of the **fertility** significance of the ritual.

The vibrant May Day festivities in Padstow link back directly to Celtic mythology and ritual. Epona was a Celtic horse goddess whose attributes included fecundity and maternity, and across Europe, wherever they settled, the **Celts** left traces of their veneration of the horse, ranging from small bronzes to the 110-metre (360-foot) chalk carving of the white horse on the hillside at Uffington. (*See* **Uffington White Horse**.)

Hurlers, The

Three **stone circles** collectively known as The Hurlers stand close together on Bodmin Moor, the name recalling a belief that the stones were men turned to stone for 'hurling the ball' on 'the Lord's Day'. They were also said to be difficult to count, but Dr Yonge in 1675 explained how that problem was solved when someone placed a loaf on each stone, a procedure also used elsewhere – presumably when a successful outcome was reached, the participants would celebrate with a sandwich lunch! (*See also* **Countless Stones**.) The Hurlers circles vary in size from 32 metres (105 feet) to 41 metres (135 feet) across, and they lie in a line. One of the circles contains an impressive diamond-shaped stone, which may symbolize the female (as opposed to the phallic male stone). In the Kennet Avenue of stones at **Avebury**, tall phallic shapes alternate with broad diamond shapes, and each faces its opposite across the avenue. This sexual symbolism may have had some importance in **fertility** rituals.

Location: 6.5 kilometres (4 miles) N of Liskeard, Cornwall. OS ref: SX 258713.

I

Inauguration stones

The best-known example is probably the Stone of Destiny which is now under the Coronation Chair in Westminster Abbey, London. It was the custom for Celtic and Saxon kings to be installed sitting or standing on an inauguration stone, and another which can be seen in the south of England is the Coronation Stone at Kingston-upon-Thames. Seven Saxon kings crowned during the 10th century sat on this stone. It was important for the king to make physical contact with the stone, and in many instances a **footprint** was carved into the stone, in which the man stood. An example of such a stone can be seen at **Dunadd** fort in Scotland. Another was the Stone of Inauguration or the Stone of the Footmarks (now destroyed) by Loch Finlaggan on Islay which was 2 metres (7 feet) square and had footprints cut into it. When a chief of Clan Donald was installed as King of the Isles he stood barefoot in the footprints with his father's sword in his hand, and was anointed by the Bishop of Argyll and seven priests.

Iona

See **Isles, sacred**

Iron Age

This followed the **Bronze Age** in Britain, and was so named because iron was used to make tools. The period began around 2,500 – 3000 years ago, and ended when the Romans gained power in Britain. The major **prehistoric sites** of the Iron Age were **hill-forts**.

Isles, sacred

Britain, itself an island, has many smaller islands dotted around it, some of which have become especially sacred places, for example Bardsey Island off the Lleyn Peninsula of Gwynedd. There was a

Celtic monastery there, and its alternative name of the Island of Twenty Thousand Saints refers to the large number of monks and pilgrims said to be buried there. Ghostly monks seen on the shore presage storms and shipwrecks. **Merlin** is said to lie sleeping on Bardsey, either in an underground chamber and surrounded by the Thirteen Treasures of Britain, or in an invisible house of glass, with nine companions. Another sacred island which really exists is Iona, off western Scotland, where many relics of early Celtic Christianity can be seen. It was St Columba who came from Ireland and founded the first monastic settlement on Iona. Followers of St Columba took Christianity south-eastwards to Northumbria, settling on **Lindisfarne** or Holy Island.

There are also numerous invisible islands around Britain, such as the Green Islands of the Sea, off south-west Wales. **Fairies** lived there, travelling to the mainland along undersea tunnels; sailors sometimes saw the islands, and the best way to do so was to stand on a turf from St David's churchyard. Tir nan Og was a legendary island, the Land of Youth, somewhere out to the west, and Hy Breasil was sometimes seen to the west of Ireland. More about the folklore of Britain's sacred islands can be found in our book *The Enchanted Land*. (*See also* **Llanddwyn Island**.)

J

Jack-in-the-Green

A figure covered in green boughs was a central character in the springtime festivities on **May Day**. Other names for him included the Green Man, Jack in the Bush, the Garland, Robin of the Wood, Robin Hood, May Man and King of the May. He embodied the idea of new life springing out of death, and may have close links with the **green man** carvings seen in churches. Traditionally, Jack-in-the-Green was covered from head to foot by a wooden or wicker-work frame of roughly cone or pyramid shape, covered with interwoven branches of greenery, flowers and ribbons so that the individual within was completely hidden, and only a peephole was left for him to see his way as he danced among the merry-makers. He still appears on Garland Day (29 May) at Castleton in Derbyshire, where he is known as the Garland King. In 1993 a Jack-in-the-Green was seen in Parliament Square, London, surrounded by hundreds of Morris dancers, all demonstrating against the Government's plans to abolish the May Day holiday.

Jarlshof

A prehistoric settlement preserved by windblown sand, similar in many ways to that at **Skara Brae**. **Bronze Age**, **Iron Age**, and later dwellings can be seen.
Location: 35 kilometres (22 miles) S of Lerwick on Shetland mainland. OS ref: HU 399095.

K

Kilmartin cairn cemetery

Five **cairns** strung out in a line make up this **Neolithic** and **Bronze Age** cemetery, a good one to visit because they are impressive examples, close together and easily accessible. The most northerly is *Glebe Cairn*, now only a huge pile of pebbles, but two stone cists were found when it was excavated last century, containing food vessels and a jet bead necklace. *Nether Largie North Cairn* is next: the **burial chamber** can be entered, and inside is a stone cist or coffin which has **cup marks** and axe-head carvings on its lid. *Nether Largie Mid Cairn* has two stone cists. *Nether Largie South Cairn* is the oldest of the five, being Neolithic: it is also the most impressive, having a large burial chamber and two stone cists. *Ri Cruin Cairn* has three stone cists, one with axe-heads carved on it. Also close by is *Temple Wood Stone Circle*, which was probably also a burial cairn: the 12-metre (40-foot) circle of stones probably surrounded a cairn which covered the now-exposed stone burial cist in the centre of the site. Spiral carvings can be seen on the base of one of the northern stones.

Location: 13 kilometres (8 miles) N of Lochgilphead; 43 kilometres (27 miles) S of Oban, Argyll. Glebe Cairn OS ref: NR 833989.

Kilpeck church

The ancient church dedicated to St Mary and St David has some Saxon parts, but mostly dates from the 12th century. Its best feature is the fine stone carving, especially the south doorway with its **green man**, and the corbels all around the outside of the building. Most notable is the best example of a Sheela-na-gig (female **exhibitionist** figure) in Britain: she may represent a Celtic **fertility** goddess, or she may have been put there simply to keep evil at bay, in the same way that phallic carvings were sometimes used. (*See* **Phallus**.) There are also more fine carvings inside the church. The overwhelming atmosphere of the site is calm and peaceful, a holy place.

Location: 13 kilometres (8 miles) SW of Hereford. OS ref: SO 444305.

King Arthur
See **Arthur, King; Glastonbury**

Knowlton Circles
Churches were often built on ancient sacred sites, places that had been of religious or ritual importance in earlier times. Knowlton in Dorset is the site of several earth circles, though only one is now clearly visible to the visitor. An earth bank 3.5 metres (12 feet) high in places still survives, and the circle is 106 metres (116 yards) in diameter. this type of structure is known as a **henge**, a ritual site similar to **Stonehenge** and **Avebury**. The so-called Central Circle contains a ruined church built in the 12th century (the tower dates from the 15th century), and together circle and church form the symbol of a cross within a **circle**.
Location: 13 kilometres (8 miles) N of Wimborne Minster, Dorset. OS ref: SU 024103.

L

Labyrinth
See **Maze**

Lanyon Quoit
Although it resembles a huge table, and in fact was also known as the Giant's Table or the Giant's Quoit, this megalithic monument is believed to have been a prehistoric **burial chamber**. The body or bodies would have been placed inside a central chamber formed from large stones, and these would then have been covered by a mound of earth which has now, after perhaps five thousand years, completely eroded away. It is puzzling that the earth covering of some prehistoric burial chambers has disappeared, while others are still well covered. A combination of factors may be responsible: exposed location, soil type, method of construction, predominant weather, and the intervention of man. As with most other quoits or dolmens, Lanyon has a huge capstone: this one is 5.5 metres (18 feet) long, and a certain degree of skill must have been called for to bring it here and raise it on top of three uprights.
Location: 2.5 kilometres (1½ miles) NW of Madron, Cornwall. OS ref: SW 430337.

Leys
Alfred Watkins set out the theory of leys in the 1920s in his classic book *The Old Straight Track,* and it was he who coined the word 'ley' to describe the alignments he discovered. ('Ley-line' so often used today is strictly speaking wrong: the alignment is a 'ley', and the line of a ley is the 'ley-line'.) The alignments were straight lines linking sites of antiquity such as **standing stones** and other **prehistoric sites, crosses, churches, holy wells,** and also certain **crossroads,** sacred **trees** and mountain tops. Although Watkins appeared to be convinced that the alignments he had discovered in his native Herefordshire were evidence of a network of trackways

criss-crossing the country and nothing more, his new way of looking at the countryside was to lead to developments beyond his wildest imaginings, developments which are still in train today.

The next major step forward was the appearance in 1969 of an inspired book, *The View Over Atlantis* by John Michell. Having studied Watkins' work and the Chinese beliefs involving **dragon** paths or *lung mei*, Michell intuitively drew together many threads into a logical pattern which has been the starting point for many people's active interest in earth mysteries over the last 25 years. During the 1970s and 1980s leys were seen by many as channels of a mysterious natural **energy**, and various methods were used to try to identify the energies present in leys and at ancient sites, but now this belief has been largely superseded. In recent years ley researchers have extended their search for the meaning of Britain's terrestrial alignments to similar phenomena overseas, and are studying 'spirit ways' in China, the *ceque* alignments of Peru, and various other ancient uses of straight lines. (*See* **Spirit lines**.) Some examples of leys, and advice on how to find and plot them, can be found in Paul Devereux's book *The New Ley Hunter's Guide*.

Lindisfarne

This island, also known as **Holy Island**, off the north-east coast of England, is linked to the mainland by a causeway, and cut off at high tide. Out of season, when the teashops and souvenir shops are quiet, you can sense the atmosphere that must have prevailed here in the 7th century, when this was one of the most important Christian centres in Anglo-Saxon England. The monastery was founded in AD 635 by St Aidan, and the monk Cuthbert became prior there in 664. He lived for some time as a hermit on St Cuthbert's Isle, a tiny island just off-shore where the ruins of a later medieval chapel can still be seen. In 676 he withdrew to the Farne Islands where he lived alone for nine years. He became bishop of Lindisfarne in 685, two years before his death. When his stone coffin in the priory church was exhumed in 698, his body was found to be incorrupt (undecayed) and the island rapidly became a cult centre, with miracles taking place at the saint's shrine.

In 875 the threat of Viking invasion caused the monks to flee with the saint's remains; they also took some of St Aidan's bones, St Oswald's head and the illuminated Lindisfarne Gospels (now in the British Museum). They eventually settled in Durham in 995 and a Saxon church was built, the forerunner of the magnificent

Romanesque cathedral we see today. Both the bones of St Cuthbert and his original coffin are still there.

Many objects from the time of St Cuthbert can be seen in Lindisfarne Museum, close to the priory ruins. The saint's ghost is said to haunt the abbey and on stormy nights he can be heard hammering on an anvil, making the 'beads' that bear his name. St Cuthbert's beads, found washed up on the shore after a storm, are in fact the fossilized remains of sea-lilies, called crinoids. A ghostly white dog has also been seen in the abbey ruins. Outside the present church lies the Petting Stone which has a **fertility** legend: it was once the custom for new brides to jump over it to ensure a fruitful marriage.

Location: In Northumberland, 96 kilometres (60 miles) N of Newcastle: the causeway leaves the mainland about 16 kilometres (10 miles) SE of Berwick-upon-Tweed. Check tide times at an information centre as the island is cut off for five hours at high tide.

Lines
See **Cursus; Leys; Spirit lines**

Llanddwyn Island
St Dwyn was a 6th-century female saint who became known as the Welsh St Valentine. She was abbess of a religious community on the island, which is off the coast of Anglesey, and after her death the place became the centre of a major pilgrimage cult. The reason why she became a patron saint of lovers can be found in a legend telling that when young, she fell in love with Maelon Dafodrill, but when she refused 'unappropriated union' with him, he abandoned her. She prayed to God to cure her of her love, and in a dream she received a liquid from him which, upon drinking it, cured her completely. Maelon also received the same potion, but he turned into a lump of ice. God also gave her three requests: her first was that Maelon should be unfrozen; her second that all her requests on behalf of true lovers should be granted, so that they would either obtain the objects of their affection, or be cured of their passion; her third that she would never wish to be married. After all three requests were granted, she became a saint, and lovers who invoked her aid were granted their desire.

The focus of the love-cult was a well, Crochan Llanddwyn, which is now a pool and can still be seen in the forest near Newborough, not far from the island. William Williams of

Llandegai, writing around 1800, describes how the well was used:

> There was a spring of clear water, now choked up by the sand, at which an old woman from Newborough always attended, and prognosticated the lovers' success from the movements of some small eels which waved out of the sides of the well, on spreading the lovers' handkerchief on the surface of the water. I remember an old woman saying that when she was a girl, she consulted the woman at this well about her destiny with respect to her husband; on spreading her handkerchief, out popped an eel from the north side of the well, and soon after another crawled from the south side, and they both met on the bottom of the well. Then the woman told her that her husband would be a stranger from the south part of Carnarvonshire. Soon after, it happened that three brothers came from that part and settled in the neighbourhood where the young woman was, one of whom made his addresses to her, and in a little time married her. So much of the prophecy I remember. This couple was my father and mother.

People would also drink from the well, or bathe in it, in hopes of achieving their desire in love. There is also a well, called Ffynnon Ddwynwen (St Dwyn's Well), on the island itself, on the cliff edge: it is a spring in a natural rock basin. This was used for **healing** purposes, and especially for getting rid of warts, leading to its other name of Ffynnon Dafaden (Wart Well).

There is a ruined medieval church in the centre of the small island, where the saint's tomb was said to have been . Sick pilgrims would sleep there in hopes of a cure, and later they slept in the saint's stone bed or *gwely*, which was where the lighthouse now stands. It was also the spot where St Dwyn died, and legend says that she was carried out to look at the sunrise for the last time, but a large rock blocked her view. An angel came and split it for her, and this divided rock can still be seen on the ridge beyond the church.

The island is a beautiful place to visit, and can be reached on foot from the Anglesey shore, only being cut off during stormy weather when the tide is especially high. (*See also* **Holy wells**.)

Location: Off SW Anglesey, Gwynedd, beyond Newborough Warren. OS ref: SW 386626.

Long barrow
See **Barrow**

Long Man of Wilmington

This chalk-cut man 70 metres (230 feet) tall is the twin of the **Cerne Abbas Giant**, in that they are the only two **hill figures** depicting human beings in Britain, but that is their only link, because the Long Man is sexless, quite different from the Giant's rampant sexuality! The Long Man holds two poles, and so may be a surveyor of some kind, but his intended identity is unknown (suggestions have included St Paul, Mohammed, King Harold, a Roman soldier, Mercury, Baldur the Beautiful, Apollo, Thor, Woden, Beowulf), as is the date of his first appearance on Windover Hill close to the village of Wilmington. According to folklore, he was a **giant** who was killed and his body outlined where he lay. A 3-kilometre (2-mile) **ley** passes through the Long Man and four other locations; for details see Paul Devereux's book *The New Ley Hunter's Guide*.

Location: 5 kilometres (3 miles) NW of Eastbourne, East Sussex. OS ref: TQ 542034.

Long Meg and Her Daughters

Long Meg was a witch, and her daughters formed her coven, the whole lot being turned to stone by the Scottish wizard Michael Scot some time in the 13th century while they were holding a Sabbat, or so the legend goes. They are also said to be uncountable, and the spell will be broken if anyone manages to count them correctly twice in succession. (*See also* **Countless stones**.) There are thought to have originally been around 70 stones, though now there are 59, forming a large oval shape. Long Meg is the tallest stone, just outside the circle, and some spiral carvings can be seen on the side that faces the circle. These are thought to mark an astronomical event. It is said that if Long Meg was ever broken, she would run with blood.

Location: 6.5 kilometres (4 miles) NE of Penrith, Cumbria. OS ref: NY 571372.

Lost lands

The coastline of Britain is changing all the time, as stormy seas erode vulnerable cliffs. Whole towns have succumbed to the encroaching water, the most striking example being Dunwich (Suffolk) which was once a major port. Now it is only a village, the town having been gradually eaten away during the last six centuries. Nine churches have been lost, and it is said that church bells can be heard ringing offshore to warn of approaching storms.

Of whole tracts of land that have been lost, the most famous must be **Lyonesse**, which once lay between Cornwall and Brittany. Wales has lost more land to the sea than any other part of Britain, and in legend some kingdoms were submerged as a punishment for evil living, or in vengeance. Some Welsh and English lakes are said to conceal drowned settlements, such as Bala Lake (Llyn Tegid) in Gwynedd. The old town of Bala was drowned because of the sinfulness of its inhabitants, according to legend. More examples of lost lands can be found in our book *The Enchanted Land*.

Lyonesse

This is a **lost land** which once existed off Cornwall, to the south and west of Land's End, but now lies beneath the sea. There is evidence that Lyonesse is not just a legend: the Scilly Isles are its hilltops, and stone walls and huts have been found below the high-water mark in the Scillies. Tree stumps from a submerged forest have been found in Mount's Bay, and St Michael's Mount, now offshore, was once called 'the ancient rock in the wood'. Lyonesse was said to have been submerged suddenly, and fishermen used to say that they could see roofs beneath the water on clear moonlit nights, and hear the church bells ringing.

M

Maes Howe passage grave

One of the finest examples of prehistoric architecture and work-manship in north-west Europe, Maes Howe dates back 4,500 to 5,000 years, being built in the **Neolithic** era by skilled craftsmen. Under a mound of stones, peat and clay lies hidden a large stone chamber with a long stone passage leading outside; small cavities in the chamber walls would have held the bones of the dead. But this was not simply a tomb; as with so many other prehistoric structures, it reveals an early preoccupation with the heavens. The passage faces south-west, and when the blocking stone which acted as a door was in place, a wide rectangular gap was left at the top – but this door was not ill-fitting: the gap had a purpose. It is very similar to the 'roof-box' above the entrance to the impressive Irish chambered tomb at Newgrange, and its purpose was also the same: to allow the last rays of the Midwinter setting **sun** to enter the tomb. This symbolic link between death and the sun demon-strates a belief in the eternal power of the life-giving sky-god: just as the sun has not died, but from that date will begin to light the earth for a longer time each day, so the ancestors whose remains lie in the tomb are not truly dead but in some magical way are eternal like the sun. (*See also* **Astronomy**.)

Location: On Orkney mainland, between Stromness and Kirkwall. OS ref: HY 318127.

Maiden Castle

There are many fine **hillforts** in Britain, but this must surely rank as one of the finest. It covers 45 acres, and the rampart is 2.5 kilome-tres (1½ miles) round the inner circumference. The banks and ditches which were dug to fortify the site are still breathtaking. Despite these defences, however, Maiden Castle was successfully invaded by the Romans in AD 43, and afterwards it was aban-doned, the people who had lived in the town inside the castle moving to the site of what is now Dorchester. A war cemetery with many human remains has been excavated by one of the gateways into the fort, and another burial site has also been found, this time inside a mound of earth around 0.5 kilometres (⅓ mile) in length which can barely be made out inside the earthworks. This may have been some kind of ritual murder: the man had been hacked to death and dismembered in Saxon times, around AD 635, long after the Roman attack. Another intriguing feature of the fort is the small Romano-Celtic temple which was built in the late 4th century AD, again after the site was abandoned. Its foundations can still be seen.

Location: Just S of Dorchester, Dorset. OS ref: SY 670885.

Markstones

These were first noted by Alfred Watkins, who discovered **leys**. They are large unworked stones – not **standing stones** – usually found by a road, in a bank or under a hedge, at **crossroads**, and thought to mark the route of a ley. They may also have been a focal point at which a market was set up, as they are sometimes found in town centres, as at Pembridge in Herefordshire where there is a clear markstone right beside the old market building.

May Day

The high point of all the spring festivals was undoubtedly May Day, which was usually held on the first of the month. On this day, throughout Europe, the **fertility** of the earth was reaffirmed and celebrated. Soon after midnight the young men and women of the community would meet and go into the woods. Their purpose was twofold: to cut down and bring home the 'maypole' tree, may blossom, and other greenery; and to practise the symbolic ritual of orgiastic mating which would cause nature to respond in kind. Such practices were opposed by the Christian Church, and eventually in 1644 the Puritans succeeded in getting the May festivities banned by Parliament. Orders were issued that all maypoles (which had by then evolved from being freshly hewn trees with lopped branches into permanently erected and decorated poles) should be destroyed by constables or other local officials, who were to be fined five shillings a week (no small sum in those times) until the maypoles were removed. But with the restoration of the monarchy in 1660, the maypole once more became a centre of festivities and many were re-erected throughout the land.

As well as decorating house exteriors and the maypole with greenery and flowers, 'mayers' would go from house to house announcing the arrival of spring with rhymes, songs and dances which varied in each district. They were rewarded with gifts of eggs, dried fruit or cake, and those who refused to give anything were warned that their crops would fail and their herds would not prosper. The mayers were led and presided over by the May Queen and King. They were a young couple chosen to epitomize the sacred marriage between sky and earth which had been consummated by many in the fields and forests the previous night. Traditionally May Day was spent in sports and pastimes, eating, drinking and dancing at the foot of the maypole, its phallic shape symbolizing the reason behind the May Day festivities. (*See* **Phallus**.) In many areas the fertility theme was also represented by a figure covered in green boughs, sometimes known as **Jack-in-the-Green**.

Today May Day is still celebrated, but rather more sedately than in past centuries. Maypole dancing is still practised, but usually by children, and the night-time orgies are (probably) a thing of the past. But in some places where the May Day festivities seem to be directly descended from pagan fertility rites, the atmosphere is still very emotive, as at Padstow in Cornwall, for example, where a man disguised as a hobby horse dances through the streets accompanied by musicians and dancers (*see* **Horse**).

Maypole
See **May Day; Phallus**

Maze
Only two forms of maze or labyrinth are widely known today – the hedge maze and the maze as a children's puzzle. But these are two relatively recent developments of an image which has been in existence, and has had a special significance for people, for several thousand years. There are two main types: if the path from the outside to the centre has no false turnings, it is 'unicursal'; if there are dead ends, or a number of routes to the centre, then it is a 'multicursal' pattern. The names 'labyrinth' and 'maze' are interchangeable, though the former is more usually applied to the ancient and symbolic forms, while 'maze' is used for a multicursal design which it is all too easy to get lost in. Labyrinths were known in pre-Christian times, and designs which are remarkably

labyrinthine in appearance can be found carved on rocks in several parts of northern Europe. Spiral carvings at prehistoric **burial chambers** may have been early labyrinths, and the banks and ditches of some **Iron Age** earthworks look labyrinthine when seen from the air. There is evidence for the existence of an early three-dimensional labyrinth on **Glastonbury** Tor in Somerset, possibly used for initiation purposes.

Spiral and labyrinth designs can be interpreted as symbols of the earth's entrails, even as symbols of the **Earth Mother** herself. To some people the spiral symbolized **water** and lunar **fertility**, and was carved on female idols, while to others it symbolized the return to the Earth Mother at death, which may be why it sometimes appears in burial chambers. Much later usages of the labyrinth idea in the form of mazes cut in the turf or built of stones may also have had a fertility significance, in that ritual dances or races through the mazes could have symbolized the rebirth of life at springtime. Documentary evidence is lacking, but May Eve games were certainly held at one turf maze, the Julian's Bower at Alkborough.

The main survival of mazes and labyrinths in England is in the form of turf mazes, of which there were once probably a great many, though less than ten now survive, simply because if they are not maintained they easily become overgrown. The survivors are the City of Troy in the Howardian Hills of North Yorkshire, Julian's Bower at Alkborough in Humberside, Wing maze in Leicestershire, Hilton maze in Cambridgeshire, Saffron Walden maze in Essex, the Troy Town at Somerton in Oxfordshire, the Mizmaze at Breamore in Hampshire and the Mizmaze on St Catherine's Hill near Winchester, Hampshire. Also worth seeing are the two tiny labyrinths carved on a rock outcrop in Rocky Valley near Tintagel, Cornwall – their date is unknown, but they could be very old. Much younger are most of the hedge mazes: new ones are being planted every year, but the oldest surviving hedge maze in England is that in the grounds of Hampton Court Palace near London, which was constructed in 1690 and may have replaced an even older maze.

Megalith

Meaning literally 'large stone', megalith is used when describing prehistoric monuments where large slabs have been used to build them, as for example in megalithic tombs.

Men-an-Tol

Literally 'stone of the hole', the Men-an-Tol might originally have been a **burial chamber**. Now there are only three sizeable stones at the site: a round **holed stone** is flanked either side by an upright pillar stone. Anyone interested in the symbolism of shapes might see here a female stone and two male phallic stones, and if you look for them you can find many examples of both phallic symbolism and male and female stones juxtaposed. (*See* **Phallus**.) Whether this is significant, or merely in the eye of the beholder, is anyone's guess!

Traditionally, people resorted to the Men-an-Tol when they wished to cure certain ailments, and the main feature of the ritual was either to crawl through the hole, or, if the patient was a child, to pass the infant through the hole. This procedure obviously symbolizes birth, the sick person being symbolically reborn to a new life without the unwanted affliction. If this site was originally a prehistoric tomb, then the hole in one of the stones may have been put there so that access could easily have been gained to an otherwise inaccessible chamber. Possibly the original builders were also aware of the tomb/womb identification and themselves performed rebirth rituals at such sites. There are other holed stones at burial chambers, including one at **Trethevy Quoit**, also in Cornwall, so in that sense the Men-an-Tol is not unique. (*See also* **Healing**.)
Location: 6.5 kilometres (4 miles) NW of Penzance, Cornwall. OS ref: SW 426349.

Menhir

Applied to **standing stones**, this means 'long stone', which is self-explanatory.

Merlin

He is best known as the wizard of Arthurian legend, but Merlin was a complex character who appears in various medieval texts. It was once thought that he was invented by the 12th-century chronicler Geoffrey of Monmouth, in whose work *The History of the Kings of Britain* his name first appears. But that now seems unlikely, because Merlin (or, in the Welsh form, Myrddin) is also referred to in early Welsh literature dating back to the 6th century.

According to Geoffrey's account, Merlin was fetched from his home in Carmarthen by Vortigern, King of the British, around the middle of the 5th century, when the king was advised to sacrifice a fatherless child and use his blood to help build a fortress in Snowdonia (**Dinas Emrys**) which had so far proved impossible, as the work continually collapsed. But the boy Merlin told Vortigern that there were two **dragons** in a pool on the site which were causing all the problems. He also prophesied future events, including the overthrow of Vortigern, which duly happened, and Aurelius took over the throne and defeated the Saxons. He wished to erect a monument commemorating slaughtered British chieftains, and Merlin was chosen as the architect. He brought over a stone circle from Ireland called the Giants' Ring and set it up at **Stonehenge**, with the help of an army led by Uther Pendragon. Merlin later helped Uther win the love of Ygraine, by changing him into an exact likeness of her husband Gorlois, Duke of Cornwall, and at their castle at **Tintagel** Uther spent the night with Ygraine and a son was conceived, who was the future King **Arthur**.

There are other versions of Merlin's life, and accounts of his activities as a wizard and prophet. Legends about him have been recorded all over the country, and there are many places claiming to be linked to him, in addition to his birthplace of Carmarthen. They include **Glastonbury**, Alderley Edge in Cheshire, Bardsey Island off Gwynedd (*see* **Isles, sacred**), and Drumelzier in southern Scotland (one of the places where his grave is said to be). A useful guidebook to Merlin sites in England, Wales, Scotland, Ireland and Brittany is *On the Trail of Merlin* by Ean Begg and Deike Rich.

Mermaid

This mythical sea enchantress is to be found in the folklore of most countries worldwide, and not least in Britain. English sea-based mermaids were mostly found living off Cornwall, the best-known being the one whose portrait can be seen on a carved bench-end in Zennor church. She captivated a young chorister and led him into the sea, and he was never seen again, though his voice could sometimes be heard in Pendour Cove as he sang to his bride beneath the sea. Some mer-folk tales claim to be factual, like the 1814 sighting of a merman off Port Gordon (Banff), and the stoning to death of a mermaid on the island of Benbecula some time in the last century.

Surprisingly, mermaids are also said to live in certain inland pools and lakes, like the one that lived in Aqualate Mere (Staffordshire) and apparently had a penchant for speaking in doggerel verse. She originally lived in Newport Mere (Shropshire), but left when it dried out, and afterwards threatened what would happen if her new home should also become uninhabitable. She appeared to workmen doing dredging work at the mere and told them: 'If this mere you do let dry, Newport and Meretown I will destr'y.' There is some overlap between the mermaids of inland waters and **fairy** women who often lived in lakes and married human men. More details of Britain's mermaids can be found in our book *The Enchanted Land*.

Merry Maidens

A stone circle in Cornwall has this name because of a story that the stones are really dancing girls turned to stone because they danced on the Sabbath. Not far away are two tall standing stones called the Pipers – the musicians who were turned to stone while trying to escape. Another standing stone close by is called the Blind Fiddler (*see* **Petrifaction**). At the roadside near the circle is Tregiffian **burial chamber**, where cremated bones and an urn were found, and a large cup-marked stone can be seen (*see* **Cup and ring marks**).
Location: 6.5 kilometres (4 miles) SW of Penzance, Cornwall; Merry Maidens in field beside B3315 road. OS ref: SW 433245.

Michael, St

See **Glastonbury; St Michael Line**

Midsummer

Midsummer Day (24 June) falls three days after the Summer Solstice, the day when the sun reaches its highest point and afterwards begins to decline. This has been seen as a significant time of the year right back into prehistory, and was one of the focal points of early astronomical experiments, presumably being marked by certain rituals at **prehistoric sites**. (*See* **Astronomy**.) In recorded history, Midsummer was a time for **fire ceremonies**, bonfires being lit, blazing tar-barrels rolled along, flaming wheels rolled down hillsides, on Midsummer Eve, supposedly with the aim of strengthening the sun as it started to decline. In addition, the fires were also intended to drive away evil spirits, and bring **fertility** to crops and people.

Mitchell's Fold stone circle

The story of a magical white cow which gave endless supplies of milk was located here. Mitchell (or Medgel) may have been the name of a **giant** who used to milk his cow at the circle. In a time of famine, she could be found waiting at the circle to give a pailful of milk to anyone who needed it. They knew that if anyone took more, the cow would never return. A bad-tempered old witch brought a sieve and milked the cow into it: of course she could not fill it, and eventually the witch milked her dry. The cow never came back; and the witch was turned into a **standing stone**, now one of those in the circle. Alternatively, she was buried in the middle of the circle so that she couldn't appear as a **ghost**. When the circle was monitored for radiation, it was found that the tallest stone, 2 metres (6 feet) tall, strongly affected the needle of a compass held against it. In August 1987, on the night of the Harmonic Convergence, a New Age event, balls of light were allegedly seen among the stones. (*See* **Earth lights**.)

Location: 1.5 kilometres (1 mile) NE of Priestweston, Shropshire. OS ref: SO 304983.

Monsters

Apart from the most famous British monster, who is of course Nessie, the creature that allegedly lives in Loch Ness near Inverness in Scotland, there are several other Scottish lakes said to be monster haunts, and even one in Wales, Lake Bala. The Scottish lakes where monsters have been reported in recent years include Shiel, Eil, Lochy, Oich and Morar, all in Inverness. The modern-day lake monsters may be simply adapted from the legendary beliefs in water-bulls and water-horses (kelpies), some of whose escapades we described in our book *The Enchanted Land*. But some may be real creatures, which perhaps came into the lochs from the sea (some Scottish lochs are sea-lochs, or are linked to the sea by waterways), because there have also been reports of monsters seen in the sea around our shores. We included a chapter on these in our book *Modern Mysteries of Britain*, in which we described some sea monsters that were actually seen on the beach. One appeared at Filey Brig in North Yorkshire in 1934, and was seen by a coast-guard. He was walking along the shore on a dark moonless night when he heard a loud growling noise ahead. Shining his torch towards it, he saw 'a huge neck, six yards ahead of me, rearing up 8 feet high!' The head was 'a startling sight – huge, tortoise eyes, like saucers, glaring at me, the creature's mouth was a foot wide and its neck would be a yard round.' The body seemed to be 9 metres (30 feet) long, with two humps, and the creature had four short legs with huge 'flappers'. It rolled itself quickly into the sea, and the coastguard saw 'two eyes like torchlights shining out to sea'.

Some water 'monsters' may well be misidentifications of normal creatures like otters, seals, or swimming deer. Some may even be as yet unknown species. And some may be unreal, or paranormal. If some water monsters, and other monsters such as **black dogs**, are some kind of paranormal manifestation, why and how are people seeing them? If there are indeed unknown **energies** at certain special sites in the landscape, it may be that sometimes a phenomenon (whatever it might be – poltergeist, **ghost**, monster, etc) can tap into these energies and materialize.

Moon
See **Sun**

Mother goddess
The female principle has been worshipped by Man for as long as he has been in existence: even the Upper Palaeolithic or Old Stone Age cave art of around 40,000 BC includes carvings of **fertility** symbols such as vulvas. The cave artists also made sculptures, some of them female figures now known collectively as 'Venus figurines' because of their shape and supposed erotic nature. Erich Neumann described them as 'representations of the pregnant goddess of fertility, who was looked upon throughout the world as the goddess of pregnancy and child-bearing, and who, as a cult object not only of women but also of men, represents the archetypal symbol of fertility and of the sheltering, protecting, and nourishing elementary character.' The best examples of Venus figurines have been found outside Britain, but a similar object is the chalk 'goddess' from Grimes Graves in Norfolk. Today deep hollows in the wild breckland show the site of the **Neolithic** flint mines which were in use between 3000 and 2500 BC. Over 360 filled-in mine shafts have been found, and one of them, 9 metres (30 feet) deep, is open to the public. In another pit close by, the miners left a chalk statuette with a chalk **phallus** and a pile of flint nodules and antler picks in front of it. The phallus and the pregnant woman suggest that the miners were trying to stimulate the **Earth Mother** into producing the 'offspring' they most desired at that place, flint. Apparently that particular mine was deficient, and was abandoned shortly after the statuette was set up.

The Romans also left behind carvings of what we now interpret as mother goddesses. A small one, 27 centimetres (11 inches) high, was found at Caerwent in Gwent, the Roman Venta Silurum, where there is evidence for a **healing** cult at a shrine there. At Cirencester in Gloucestershire (the Roman Corinium Dobunnorum) a carved trio of goddesses showed how the Romans often honoured 'the mothers' or 'Matres'. They hold fruits and other foodstuffs, and clearly symbolize the fertility of the earth. The woman as mother and life-giver has always been a powerful image, and mother-goddess images would have been used to invoke the qualities of fertility and fruitfulness which she embodied.

Mousa broch

The best-preserved example of a **broch**, or prehistoric fortified tower, is in the Shetland islands: its stone tower still stands 12 metres (40 feet) high. A stairway rises clockwise inside the hollow wall to the top of the tower, the fine detail of its structure showing that it was built by a master craftsman. Probably a very important chieftain lived there.

Location: On Mousa island, Shetland. OS ref: HU 457237.

Moving stones

Some **standing stones** were very difficult to move: farmers would try to move them, using horses and chains, but be unable to shift them: one was the Wimblestone at Shipham in the Mendip Hills (Somerset). But at night the stone would roam around the Mendips! Other stones, said to conceal **treasure**, were also impossible to move; or, as in the case of the Caractacus Stone on Exmoor (Somerset), it fell on top of a waggoner who tried to move it, crushing him to death. When the capstone of the **burial chamber** called the Whispering Knights close to the **Rollright Stones** was taken for use as a bridge, several horses were needed to drag it downhill; but when the farmer decided to return it to its rightful place, only one horse was needed to pull it back uphill again.

Some stones were believed to be able to return 'home' if taken away, like the magic stone which bears the **footprint** of King **Arthur**'s dog, Cabal, on the Powys mountain Cefn Carn Cabal, or the Thigh Stone (Maen Morddwyd) on the island of Anglesey which always returned the next night. Once it was chained to a larger stone and thrown into the sea, but next morning it was back in its usual place.

79

The Dancing Stones of Stackpole (Dyfed) are an example of stones which were said to be able to move about: these would dance the hay (a country-dance), and good luck was said to visit anyone who witnessed it. Some stones go down to the nearest pool or stream to drink, such as the Four Stones at Old Radnor (Powys) and the Giant's Stone at Yetnasteen on Rousay (Orkney). Other human characteristics possessed by some stones were washing, eating and growing. More examples of moving stones can be found in our book *The Secret Country*. (*See also* **Cock-crow stones**.)

N

Neolithic

From the New Stone Age, dating roughly from 4000 to 2000 BC, almost 4000-6000 years ago. During this time the first lasting structures were created: **burial chambers** made from large slabs of stone and covered with mounds of earth. **Henges**, such as **Avebury** and **Stonehenge**, probably also date from the Stone Age.

Nevern

The church here was founded by the 6th-century St Brynach, who lived as a hermit on the nearby mountain Carn Ingli and communed with the angels (*see* **Preseli Hills**). There are numerous interesting features to see around the church, the most notable of which is the fine Celtic cross in the churchyard. This dates from the late 10th or early 11th century and is 4 metres (13 feet) tall. Front, back and sides are all decorated with interlaced patterns. According to tradition, the first cuckoo perches on St Brynach's Cross to sing on 7 April, the saint's feast-day. By the church porch is another stone, with a Latin inscription dating from the 5th-6th century. It also has some **Ogham** writing carved on it, as does another stone to be found inside the church in a window-sill. The churchyard has numerous old, dark, yew trees, from one of which drips a dark-red sap, giving it the name of the Bleeding Yew. Above the church is an old pilgrim path, where a wayside cross has been cut into the rockface.

Location: 11 kilometres (7 miles) SW of Cardigan, Dyfed. OS ref: SN 083401.

O

Offerings

There are numerous examples in folklore of offerings being made to **standing stones**. This custom may be behind the belief that the stones at certain circles were countless, and loaves of bread were placed on them in an effort to reach an accurate total. (*See also* **Countless stones**.) But there is also more direct evidence for the leaving of offerings. In Scotland milk was poured into cup markings and natural hollows in stones, until the early years of this century. (*See* **Cup and ring marks**.) The offerings were made to the Gruagach, 'the hairy one', a cattle guardian, and if they were forgotten or ignored, things would go wrong, the cattle would fall ill and die.

In other cases, the offerings took the form of flowers, or food-stuffs. Cakes of barley-meal, honey and milk were left on Arthur's Stone on the Gower peninsula of South Wales at midnight when there was a full moon, by young girls who would crawl round the stone three times on hands and knees. They hoped to see their sweethearts: if they appeared, the girls knew they were faithful; if not, then the girls knew that the boys did not intend marriage.

Some offerings give a hint of earlier **sacrifice**, maybe animal, perhaps even human. At Holne in Devon, on **May Day** morning, a live ram was tied to a granite stone and its throat cut, the blood flowing over the stone. Then the whole animal was roasted, and the people would scramble for slices of the meat, which was believed to confer good luck. (*See also* **Witchcraft**.)

Ogham (or Ogam)

A strange script which consists of groups of parallel lines positioned over a base line: usually carved on stone, with the base line being the edge of the stone slab. It is found in the Celtic areas of the west, and may have begun as a secret script in the 3rd century AD in Ireland or South Wales. It was usually used to commemorate the dead on memorial pillar stones.

Old Sarum

The deep ditch of the **Iron Age hillfort** is the first feature one notices when walking into Old Sarum. Inside the Romans had a settlement, then the Saxons took it over, and later a Norman castle was built, whose ruins are still considerable. A cathedral was founded here in the 11th century, but 200 years later it was abandoned and a new cathedral founded not far away where Salisbury Cathedral stands today. At Old Sarum the foundations of the old cathedral and crypt of the chapter house can still be seen. The church within the protecting **circle** together form a powerful symbol, repeated countrywide in churches sited within circular churchyards. A **ley** also passes through Old Sarum: 30 kilometres (18½ miles) long, it also takes in a **tumulus**, **Stonehenge**, Salisbury Cathedral, Clearbury Ring hillfort and Frankenbury Camp hillfort. Further details can be found in Paul Devereux's book *The New Ley Hunter's Guide*.

Location: Close to Salisbury, Wiltshire. OS ref: SU 1332.

P

Padstow hobby horse
See **Horse**

Paganism
From the Latin *paganus*, meaning countryman, paganism refers to a non-Christian religion, or nature-worship, with gods and goddesses to be found in all the natural elements of earth, air, fire, water, in the trees and rivers, woods and wells. So far as Christianity was concerned, pagans were unenlightened barbarians, and anyone not embracing Christianity was automatically a pagan, and liable to persecution, which may help to explain why witches were persecuted during the Middle Ages.

Pentre Ifan
This elegant **cromlech**, with a 5-metre (16½-foot) capstone seemingly delicately balanced 2.5 metres (8 feet) above the ground on top of its supporting uprights, is believed to have once been a **burial chamber**, constructed in the **Neolithic** period up to 6,000 years ago. What amazing secrets do those old stones conceal? All we know about the place now is that it is supposed to be a **fairy** haunt: they looked like 'little children in clothes like soldiers' clothes and with red caps', said one person who saw them.
Location: 11 kilometres (7 miles) SW of Cardigan, Dyfed. OS ref: SH 099370.

Petrifaction
Some of the **stone circles** and **standing stones** in Britain have strange names, such as the **Merry Maidens**, the Pipers, the Blind Fiddler, the **Hurlers**, and **Long Meg and Her Daughters**. These refer to folk stories that tell how the stones are really people who were turned to stone, or petrified, for some transgression, often dancing or working on a Sunday. Other sites have similar stories

attached to them, even though this is not reflected in the familiar name. Another name for **Stonehenge** was Chorea Gigantum, or the Giants' Dance, according to a 12th-century scholar, and this suggests that at one time the huge stones were seen as petrified giants.

The story of how the stones at the prehistoric site of Stanton Drew (Avon) came to be there is one of the most detailed. The main group of stones was called the Weddings, and a separate group of three large stones was said to be the parson, bride and bridegroom. The wedding was held on a Saturday and the celebrations continued until late at night, almost into Sunday. The fiddler refused to continue playing after midnight, but a dark-clad stranger suddenly appeared and began to play. The music went faster and faster, and the dancers couldn't stop. At dawn, the **Devil** (who was of course the fiddler) stopped playing and told the dancers he would return some day and play for them again. Until that day comes, they must remain as stones.

Sometimes a stone's appearance would suggest a story and a name, like the Saddle Stone on the Isle of Man, said to be a vicar's saddle used by the **fairies** one night and then turned to stone; or the Sack Stone in Lincolnshire, which was said to be a sack of corn turned to stone by Christ. In Oxfordshire a group of stones looks just like a huddle of men, and the name they now have, the Whispering Knights, is explained in a story involving a whole complex of stones at **Rollright**.

The vivid imaginations of the country people, seeking to explain strange features on the landscape, will account for most of the petrifaction stories, but some, like the stories of dancers and the Devil, may have arisen after people saw witches dancing at stone circles or performing magic rituals while dressed in strange costumes (*see* **Witchcraft**).

There are also a few petrifying wells in Britain, where articles suspended in the flow of water for a few months will apparently be turned to stone. What actually happens is that the objects become encrusted in a mineral, usually calcite (a form of calcium carbonate), which builds up in layers. The most famous is the Dripping or Dropping Well at Knaresborough, North Yorkshire.

Phallus
Some **standing stones** may have symbolized the male and female principles, stones of phallic shape symbolizing the male, and holed

stones or diamond stones symbolizing the female. The two are seen together at the **Men-an-Tol**, where two phallic stones stand either side of a roughly circular **holed stone**. Also at **Avebury**, male and female stones are seen in the Kennet Avenue, and at **Stonehenge** the phallic bluestones stand surrounded by the female trilithons. When looking for male and female stones, one begins to see them everywhere, especially phallic stones. Most standing stones are tall, narrow pillars, but that does not necessarily mean that they were intended as phallic symbols. However, when a standing stone has been deliberately shaped so that it is topped by a knob strongly resembling the glans of a penis, then there is little doubt what was intended by the erector. Being so explicit, stones like this have been damaged or destroyed, and the best surviving example in this part of the world is in Ireland.

Not only standing stones may carry phallic symbolism. The upright Christian **cross** developed from the standing stone, and some of the older crosses are decidedly phallic in shape, with no arms, just a tall shaft ending in a knob. Also church spires are sometimes phallic in appearance, especially the oldest ones: but care must be exercised, as such interpretations may be strictly in the eye of the beholder and never intended by the creators of these apparently phallic objects!

Certainly clear in intention are the phalluses carved on to stones. There is a beautiful one on a paving stone in the courtyard of the headquarters building at Chesters Roman fort in Northumberland, and others at other Roman sites, because the Romans used the phallus as a good luck sign and it may have been used to counteract evil. In the early 1990s another good example was discovered in a newly ploughed field at Llangwm in Gwent, South Wales. The carving goes over the edge of the stone to show what is probably a flow of semen. It is thought that the stone was a keystone, possibly from a well or spring. This suggested link between the phallus and a water source shows its use in a **fertility** context: maybe this well was famed for its cure for barrenness? (*See also* **Holy wells**.)

Also strongly linked to fertility, the maypole may also be a phallic symbol: certainly the night-time fetching of the tree which was originally used as a maypole at **May Day** celebrations was allegedly accompanied by orgiastic mating among the young men and women of the community who went down to the woods together. During the recent excavation of what appears to have been an astronomical temple at Godmanchester near Cambridge, 24 wooden obelisks were discovered. The alignment of the two largest pointed towards the place on the horizon where the sun rose on May Day, and it is possible that the obelisks represented phallic pillars and thus were the forerunners of the maypole, not previously thought to have existed before Saxon times.

Pictish symbol stones

The Picts were a Scottish tribe living in the north-east of the country around AD 300-850. The early symbol stones were **standing stones** on which the Picts carved designs like mirrors, combs, snakes, animals, birds, fishes. The designs became more elaborate after AD 700, and were carved on to stones shaped like Christian **crosses**. These can be compared with the **Celtic** crosses that are found mainly in Wales and Ireland. Some of the symbols that the Picts used are difficult to identify. One animal, somewhat elephant-like, may represent a water **monster** like the Loch Ness Monster. All the animals the Picts carved were ones familiar to them – wolf, bull, cow, stag, horse, eagle, goose – so maybe they were also familiar with water monsters. Pictish symbol stones can be seen in many locations; there are some excellent examples at Aberlemno (Angus) and also in the Meigle Museum (Perth).

Prehistoric sites

'Prehistory' is the time before man developed writing to record events; our knowledge of man's life in prehistory has to be deduced from what he left behind in the way of artefacts and structures. In Britain, prehistory is roughly the time before the Romans invaded (AD 43), and still-surviving visible evidence stretches back about 4000 years before that, to c.4000 BC when the **Neolithic** or new Stone Age began, and the first **megalithic** tombs and long barrows were built. The **Stone Age** was followed by the **Bronze Age** and then the **Iron Age**. Prehistoric sites described in this book are: **barrow, burial chamber, cromlech, cairn, dolmen, henge, hillfort, quoit, standing stone, stone circle, tumulus**, and a list of prehistoric sites to visit is given on page 123.

Preseli Hills

This is a magical area with a number of significant locations. They include: *Gors Fawr stone circle*, with 16 stones making a circle 22 metres (72 feet) in diameter. Two 2-metre (6-foot) stones a short distance away to the north-east form an alignment marking the **midsummer** sunrise over Preseli.

Carn Meini, rocky outcrops high on Preseli, are thought to be the source of the bluestones at **Stonehenge.**

Carn Ingli, a rocky peak with tumbled stone walls from early forts, possibly dating from the **Iron Age**. The name means 'Peak of Angels', and this refers to the 6th-century St Brynach, who lived as a hermit on the peak, and talked to the angels who kept him company. The major church he founded was at **Nevern** not far away. Strong magnetic anomalies have been noted on the hilltop, and it was chosen for the site of a **dream research** programme.

Frenifawr, a hill in the Preselis, was a **fairy** haunt. A shepherd lad one day saw fairies dancing on the hill, and went up to watch them, eventually joining in their circle. He found himself in a beautiful palace, where he could have everything he wanted – on condition that he did not drink from a certain well in the middle of the garden. Eventually, overcome with curiosity, he did drink from the well, and immediately the palace vanished and he was back on the hill with his sheep. He thought he had been gone for some years, but it proved to have been only a few minutes.

Pentre Ifan cromlech is also in this area.

Location: The Preseli hills are in Dyfed, 24 kilometres (15 miles) NW of Carmarthen. OS refs: Gors Fawr – SN 135294. Carn Meini – SN 144325. Carn Ingli – SN 063373. Freni Fawr – SN 202350.

Q

Quartz

A crystalline mineral with piezo-electric properties, which means that it can produce an electric current when put under tension or pressure. It is not uncommon, and granite usually contains 20-40 per cent quartz, so that it is usually present in **standing stones** and **stone circles**. But its presence is not always accidental: sometimes large quartz stones were clearly chosen, as for example at Boscawen-Un stone circle in Cornwall, where there is a quartz stone, and Duloe stone circle also in Cornwall, where all the stones are of white quartz, and on the Isle of Man, where the White Lady of Ballafreer is a white quartz pillar 2 metres (6-7 feet) high. In addition, white quartz pebbles have often been found scattered at **burial chambers** and **stone circles**. Offerings of white or quartz stones were made at **holy wells**, such as Ffynnon Degla (Clwyd) and Ffynnon Gwenfaen, Anglesey (Gwynedd), and charms of quartz and rock crystals were used to give the water of **healing** wells a magical potency.

Quartz was clearly a magical stone, but whether it was any more than this remains debatable. In view of its electrical properties, and its frequent use at burial sites, is it too far-fetched to suggest that prehistoric people used it in rituals to communicate with the dead, perhaps in the way mediums today claim to make contact with the 'Other Side'? Perhaps its presence was found to facilitate such practices, and so it was used in various other esoteric ceremonies, accounting for its widespread presence at stone circles too. (*See also* **Crystals**.)

Quoit

Also called a **cromlech** or **dolmen**, this was a stone **burial chamber** covered by a capstone; good examples are **Lanyon Quoit** and **Trethevy Quoit** in Cornwall, and numerous other fine quoits still survive in Britain.

R

Rain

Rain is one of the necessities for a successful crop, but all too often it falls when unwanted and is absent when the need is desperate. The vital fluid from above, sent by the sky father to fertilize the **earth mother**, sometimes had to be encouraged to fall, and rain-making ceremonies are known from many parts of the world. In the British Isles such ceremonies often involved water-sprinkling, perhaps with the intention of encouraging the rain by example. Anyone standing on the stepping-stones in Tarn Dulyn in Snowdonia, North Wales, could be sure of rain before nightfall if he threw water on to the farthest stepping-stone. In the Hebrides, the Water Cross on the island of Uist could be raised when rain was needed, and lowered when sufficient had fallen. Witches were believed to be able to produce rain at will, but it was said that they usually did this as an evil act and rarely because the farmers needed it. In some areas the cutting or burning of ferns (or heather) was believed to cause rain to fall. Farmers also relied on springs and wells for their water supply, and frequently performed special rituals at the wells. One which was once widespread and still survives strongly in Derbyshire today is the custom of **well-dressing** when the wells are decorated with flowers. (*See also* **Holy wells; Water**.)

Recumbent stone circles

There are around 80 of these, all in north-east Scotland: each small circle (often of 10 stones) has a large stone lying on edge, flanked by two tall stones, making up the circle. These circles seem to have connections with prehistoric **astronomy**, and it has been suggested that the astronomer-priests used them as astronomical observatories and could predict when the moon would appear to be travelling along the top of the recumbent stone, thus wielding great power over the naive peasantry who believed the priests to be actually controlling the moon. Rituals and ceremonies were probably also practised at the circles, maybe involving death cults as many of them also contain burial **cairns** made of stones.

Rituals
See **Customs**

Rollright Stones
Three separate prehistoric sites make up the Rollright Stones: The King's Men form a large **stone circle** with about 70 stones looking like huge rotten teeth. The Whispering Knights half a mile down the road is a group of five large stones which once formed a **burial chamber;** while across the road is the King Stone, a 2.5 metre (8 foot) tall **standing stone**. As their names suggest, these stones were once men, according to folklore. They were a king and his army, who were marching across country when they were met by a witch, who told the king:

Seven long strides thou shalt take,
And if Long Compton thou canst see,
King of England thou shalt be.

His knights stood together in a huddle, and his soldiers waited close by, as the king strode out to fulfil the prophecy. In excitement he cried:

Stick, stock, stone!
As King of England I shall be known!

But his view was blocked by the Archdruid's Barrow (a mound now almost lost by ploughing), and the witch spoke again:

As Long Compton thou canst not see,
King of England thou shalt not be,
Rise up stick, and stand still stone,
For King of England thou shalt be none.
Thou and thy men hoar stones shall be,
And myself an eldern-tree.

And so, like various other unfortunates before and since, if folklore is to be believed, they suffered the fate of **petrifaction**.

Other beliefs have arisen concerning the stones. One was that the King's Men couldn't be counted. A baker who tried to place a loaf on each stone, failed to count them because he didn't have enough loaves! (See Countless stones.) People used to chip bits off the King Stone to keep as good luck charms, and once a year youngsters would gather near the stone to dance, eat cakes and drink ale. On Midsummer Eve people would stand in a circle around the stone as part of an ancient ceremony. The King Stone also had the power of movement: he would move his head when the elder tree (the witch) was cut and bled, and he went to drink at a nearby spring when the clock struck midnight. In more recent times, the King's Men have been the venue for witchcraft rituals, and have also been monitored as part of the Dragon Project. (For more details, see Paul Devereux's book Places of Power.)

Location: 5 kilometres (3 miles) NW of Chipping Norton, Oxfordshire. OS ref: SP 296308.

Round barrow
See **Barrow**

Round Table

King **Arthur** and his knights are supposed to have sat at the Round Table, and there is a painted oak table in Castle Hall at Winchester that dates back at least to the 15th century, and is probably earlier. It is 5.5 metres (18 feet) across and divided into 24 segments, and the names of the knights are around the rim, with Arthur's place at the top. The table's origins are shrouded in mystery.

There are at least five other round tables, though none is a piece of furniture. They include the Roman amphitheatre at Caerleon (Gwent), two *Bwrdd Arthur* in Wales (*bwrdd* = table) (a hillfort near Beaumaris in Anglesey and a rocky hillside formation in Clwyd), the **henge** called Arthur's Round Table at Mayburgh (Cumbria), and an earthwork in a medieval garden at Stirling Castle in Scotland.

Rudston Monolith

The tallest **standing stone** in Britain at 7.8 metres (25 feet 9 inches) and originally even taller before its top was damaged, this stone may have stood here for 4,000 years, being set into place long before the church beside which it now stands was built. The name may come from 'rood (cross) stone', and so when the Christians took over the site they may have topped the stone with a **cross**, in order perhaps to exorcize the paganism which the stone represented. The stone must have been somehow brought 16 kilometres (10 miles) from the nearest source of this particular gritstone, but why so much trouble should have been taken to bring it to this place, we can no longer know. A local tradition says that it was the **Devil** who placed it here, throwing it at the church in order to destroy it, and fortunately missing.

Location: In Rudston churchyard, 8 kilometres (5 miles) W of Bridlington, Humberside. OS ref: TA 098677.

Runes

Runic script originated in Scandinavia, and was in active use between the 5th and 11th centuries AD. There are about 65 runic inscriptions known from Anglo-Saxon Britain, and some are very short. The longest is that which can still be seen on the **cross** inside Ruthwell church (Dumfries). This fine cross dates from the late 7th century, and various Christian scenes are depicted on it. Down the edges of the side panels, part of the text of the Anglo-Saxon poem 'Dream of the Rood' is carved in runes. Apart from a few examples such as this and a few others in south-west Scotland, most of the British examples are in the north and east of England. Runes were also carved on portable personal objects such as rings and swords. Mysterious in origin, runes may have started as a magical script. Details of rune magic can be found in medieval Scandinavian manuscripts, and in one poem a sorcerer boasts of his magical powers, including bringing people back from the dead. He says: 'If I see a corpse swaying in its noose in the tree-tops, I cut a spell, coloured in runes, so that the man will walk again and talk with me.' Runes were also used for divination and fortune-telling, and still are today.

S

Sacred sites

These are special places in the landscape, noted as such many centuries ago and chosen as the location for **prehistoric sites** such as **stone circles, standing stones, burial chambers, henges, hill-forts**. Their special nature may result from the configuration of the natural landscape features – the hills and valleys, streams and rivers – and also from the flow of natural **energy** within the landscape. Following on from their use in prehistoric times, successive generations have continued to mark the sacred sites by building their own structures, such as churches, there, and it is alignments of these sacred sites that were noted by Alfred Watkins and called by him **leys**. (*See also* **Feng-shui**.)

Sacrifice

Although there is little direct evidence of human sacrifice in Britain, it was probably performed in the distant past: the early farmers must have felt that they had good reason to perform sacrifices. They were part of the farmers' efforts to perpetuate the cycle of death and rebirth: by giving their life-spirit, the sacrificed person or animal would enrich the natural life, and thus strengthen the vegetation and crops. There are British customs which hint of sacrifice. In the Worcestershire hopfields, on the last day of hop-picking, the foreman and a woman were buried under hops in one of the baskets in which they were collected, and then the two were resurrected by being tipped out. This may have been a relic of a sacrifice aimed at ensuring a good harvest next year, similar to the ritual of the Corn Maiden, in which the last sheaf of the harvest, personified and maybe dressed like a young girl, was ritually killed, in place of a living victim, in order to restore life to the corn spirit and ensure the continuance of the agricultural cycle.

Archaeologists have found evidence suggestive of prehistoric sacrifice, for example at ritual sites and long **barrows** in Wiltshire where skulls were discovered which showed severe injury almost certainly inflicted before death. In Britain, sacrifice became 'toned down' to blood-letting, which was thought to be nearly as efficacious since blood contains the life-essence. So shedding blood does not necessarily signify taking life, but giving it. Although human sacrifice was discontinued, animal sacrifice was still practised until quite recently. On the Isle of Man there were cases in the 19th century of farmers with sick cattle sacrificing one in the hope that this would cause the others to be restored to health.

Some of the traditional **customs** still practised in Britain appear to include traces of the ritual sacrifice of the divine victim. Mummers' plays have a clear theme of death and resurrection in the killing of St George and his magical revival. Sword dances were originally also part of mummers' plays, and they too contain a ritual killing. The fool is the sacrificial victim in the Haxey Hood Game (Lincolnshire): 'Smoking the Fool' involves lighting a pile of damp straw at his feet as he makes a welcoming speech, and originally he used to be suspended from a tree and swung backwards and forwards through the smoke from the fire below. These events give clear indications of a ritual sacrifice by fire, which probably originally took place on the mid-winter solstice. (*See* **Fire ceremonies**.)

The chalking of a human figure on the Yule log before it was burnt was possibly also a remnant of human sacrifice at the mid-winter solstice. The burning of effigies of witches during the last century, particularly in Scotland, may also have stemmed from a practice which originally provided both a sacrificial victim and a means of destroying evil powers. Today it is difficult to understand how ritual sacrifice could have been condoned but it is evident that at one time throughout the world there was a generally held belief that sacrifice was essential if the well-being of the land and its peoples was to be secured.

St Cybi's Well

A group of ruined stone buildings marks the site of a once-thriving **holy well**. On the right when approaching can be seen the remains of a cottage for the custodian, built about 1750. On its left is an older building, but no earlier than the 12th century, which encloses the main pool; the actual well is hidden away behind. This was once an important **healing** centre, dating back to the time of St Cybi in the mid-6th century. The water was reputed to cure warts, lameness, blindness, scrofula, scurvy and rheumatism. At one time an eel lived in the well, and anyone seeking a cure would consider it a good sign if the eel coiled round his legs as he stood in the water. Young girls would also use the well for love divination. They would spread a handkerchief on the water and if it moved to the south, they knew that the lover's intentions were honourable; but the contrary if it moved to the north.

Location: At Llangybi (8 kilometres) 5 miles NE of Pwllheli, Gwynedd; approached along a path through the churchyard and across a field into the valley. OS ref: SH 427413.

St Govan's Chapel

The location of this tiny chapel below the cliffs, reached by a long flight of stone steps, must surely be one of the most dramatic in Britain, especially when the sea is crashing on to the rocks, and it is easy to imagine a hermit deciding to settle here. Whether St Govan was a hermit, no one knows; indeed no one knows whether he even existed. He might have been Govan, a disciple of St Ailbe, an early 6th-century bishop; or he might have been **Gawain** whose story figures in the Arthurian tradition. Gawain was believed to have been buried on the Pembrokeshire coast, and Govan/Gawain's tomb is said to be under the altar in St Govan's Chapel. The altar and a rock seat may be parts of a 5th or 6th century hermitage, though the chapel we see today is thought to date from the 13th century.

According to legend, the steps down the cliffs are said to be uncountable, and a cleft in the rock inside the chapel (in the east wall) is said to have opened up miraculously in order to conceal Govan from pirates, and closed around him until they had gone. It still bears the impression of his body – or alternatively, it concealed Jesus and bears the impression of his body. In this version, Jesus was being pursued by Jews and ran through a field where men were sowing barley. He told them to fetch their reaping hooks, and if anyone came asking for him they were to say that he had passed by at sowing time. They went to fetch their hooks and when they returned they found a field of full-grown barley ready for harvesting. A wish made while standing in the cleft facing the wall will be granted before the end of the year, if you do not change your mind as you turn around. It is said that anybody can squeeze into the cleft, because it changes size to fit you.

Another legend describes how the chapel bell was stolen and

then brought back by a miracle, but hidden inside rock. As a result, the rock of the cliff face is said to sound like a bell when struck – if you know which rock to strike. Before it was stolen, the bell sometimes used to ring without being touched, and this foretold trouble at sea or a local death. There is also a 'Huntsman's Leap' – a place where a man on horseback leapt across the chasm in order to retrieve his soul which he had sold to the Devil. St Govan blessed his horse before the attempt.

There is a small **holy well** a short distance below the chapel. Water no longer flows in it, but it was once famed for its curative properties and was much visited, some who came on crutches being able to walk away without them.

Location: 1.5 kilometres (1 mile) S of Bosherston 6.5 kilometres (4 miles) S of Pembroke), Dyfed. OS ref: SR 967929.

St Keyne's Well

Cornwall is the county where the most **holy wells** can still be found, and it is difficult to select just one to represent them all, but this is easily accessible, and has an amusing story. It was believed that the first partner of a newly married couple to drink the water would be the dominant partner in the marriage. The story was told in a poem by Robert Southey about a man who hurried to the well after his wedding in order to drink the water first, so that he would be 'Master for life'. But he was too late:

I hasten'd as soon as the wedding was done,
And left my Wife in the porch;
But, i'faith, she had been wiser than me,
For she took a bottle to Church.

Location: Just S of St Keyne, 3 kilometres (2 miles) S of Liskeard, beside a lane. OS ref: SX 248602.

St Michael Line

This is an alignment of St Michael sites and other important ancient sites, a gigantic **ley** stretching 300 miles from the furthest west to the furthest east points of England, from the rocky promontory of Carn Les Boel in Cornwall to the ruined St Margaret's church at Hopton in Norfolk, and taking in along the way St Michael's Mount, The **Hurlers** stone circles, St Michael's church on Brentor, **Glastonbury**, **Avebury**, Dorchester, and Bury St

Edmunds Abbey, among other places. Over a period of two years in the 1980s, dowser Hamish Miller and author Paul Broadhurst followed the line, tracking the current of **energy** that flows along it, and the results of their journey can be found in their book *The Sun and the Serpent*.

St Michael's Mount
See **Giants; Lyonesse; St Michael Line**

St Non's Well
In a beautiful cliff-top location, this **holy well** has a small rounded stone building over it. A few yards away across a field is the ruined St Non's Chapel, with around it a few scant remains of a **stone circle**. It was clearly once a place of importance. Legend tells how St Non (or St Nonna) came here in the 6th century on a day when a storm was raging, but she found summer weather, with sunlight and blue skies, within the stone circle. She gave birth to St David here, near the well, and from that time the waters were said to have **healing** powers. A nearby stone was said to bear the mark of St Non's hand, when she pressed down hard upon it during her delivery. (*See also* **Footprints**.) For centuries the well was visited for healing purposes, and offerings left in the water.
Location: On the outskirts of St David's, Dyfed, beside a lane leading S to St Non's Bay. OS ref: SM 751243.

St Winefride's Well
The story of how this well came into existence features a severed head, and so may be linked to a possible **head-cult**. St Winefride lived around AD 700 in North Wales, daughter of a Welsh chieftain and niece of St Beuno. One day while at home alone, she was visited by Prince Caradog, who tried to rape her. She fled in terror, and as she reached the church the enraged Caradog struck off her head with his sword. Where the head fell, water began to flow from the ground. St Beuno came from the church and cursed Caradog, who died on the spot. St Beuno replaced Winefride's severed head on to her shoulders, breathed into her nostrils, and prayed for her life. She revived and was healed, the only reminder being a thin line round her neck, which can be seen on depictions of the saint. The well became an important place of pilgrimage, a Gothic chapel was built above it, and a large bathing pool was made to accommodate the many pilgrims who came (and still

come) to seek **healing**. Many cures have been recorded. In 1606 Sir Roger Bodenham visited the well and obtained instant relief from a painful disease of the feet, after every known medical remedy had been tried, and in 1805 a paralysed servant girl named Winefred White was cured after a pilgrimage to the well. It is still an active place of pilgrimage and healing.

Location: At Holywell, Clwyd. OS ref: SJ 185763.

Samhain

This was a pre-Christian festival, celebrated on 31 October/1 November: it was a time when the curtain between this world and the Otherworld could be lifted, and powerful spiritual forces were abroad. The Christians supplanted it by harvest festival, and it was also All Saints Day, preceded by Hallowe'en which was when the dead came back from the grave, and **ghosts** and spirits walked. Divination was also practised, to try and see into the future. Ritual fires were lit, to counteract the evil spirits then at large. These are now the 5 November bonfires, which are still so popular. The fireworks would originally have been intended to frighten away the evil spirits. (*See also* **Fire ceremonies**.)

Serpent

The serpent is a lunar symbol, also connected with woman and fecundity, though the link is complex, and it also symbolizes energy. Indeed in its **dragon** form it was intimately bound up with the lore of earth energies. 'Serpent energy' may have been symbolized on the ground by the construction of serpentine avenues, such as those believed to have formerly existed at **Avebury**, and along these avenues the people would once have processed, generating energy (as in serpentine dances) as they moved toward the **stone circles** where they may then have engaged in powerful **fertility** rites. The serpent symbolized sexual energy, as is clearly shown by a stone dating from the early 3rd century, found in the cemetery of the Roman fort at Maryport in Cumbria. It is 1 metre (3-4 feet) tall and shaped like a **phallus**, with a human face on the glans, and on the reverse a serpent snakes its way up the phallus.

Sheela-na-gig
See **Exhibitionist**

Silbury Hill

At 40 metres (130 feet) high, this is the largest man-made prehistoric mound in Europe. The base covers over 5 acres, and the flat top is 30 metres (100 feet) across. Constructed around 2500 BC, archaeologists have calculated that it took 18 million man-hours to build – but why? Assuming it must be a gigantic burial mound, they have more than once during the last 200 years tunnelled into it to try and find a burial, but none has been found. According to folklore, and obviously taking the name literally, it was the burial-place of King Sil, who sits inside on horseback wearing golden armour; in another version he is in a golden coffin. Nearly 100 years ago one Moses B. Cotworth suggested that Silbury was 'a gigantic sundial to determine seasons and the true length of the year', with a large pole being erected on top and its shadow used for the calculations. More recently, Michael Dames has interpreted Silbury and the moat-like surroundings as the pregnant Great Goddess, the hill being her womb. She is a Neolithic **Earth Mother**, squatting and ready to give birth. (Dames' theory is worked out in his book *The Silbury Treasure: The Great Goddess Rediscovered*.) A **ley** passes through Silbury Hill, linking it with **Avebury** and other sites including Marden Henge; full details are given in Paul Devereux's book *The New Ley Hunter's Guide*.

Location: 8 kilometres (5 miles) W of Marlborough, Wiltshire, not far from **Avebury** and **West Kennet Long Barrow**. OS ref: SU 100685.

Skara Brae

Around 3,000 years ago, a storm blew sand over a coastal settlement in the Orkney islands; the houses lay buried until 1850 when another storm uncovered them again. The small huts contained furniture made of stone, and a picture of the inhabitants' way of life has been built up from the objects they left when they escaped from the storm. Another sand-covered settlement was found at **Jarlshof** on Shetland mainland.

Location: On Orkney mainland, 11 kilometres (7 miles) N of Stromness. OS ref: HY 231188.

Souterrain

A Scottish term for a **fogou**.

South Cadbury Castle

This fine Iron Age **hillfort** is well worth visiting for many reasons: the impressive banks and ditches, the fine views – and the strong suspicion that it may have been the site of King **Arthur's** Camelot, his main dwelling place. Its history began in **Neolithic** times, when it was first occupied; it was only during the **Iron Age** around 500 BC, that banks and ditches and ramparts were constructed. The Romans attacked in the early years AD, and then the fortress was left empty for a few hundred years, before being reoccupied in the 5th century AD. Timber buildings were constructed, including a large wooden hall as if for an important chief: King Arthur? The hill was strongly defended with timber walls on top of stone ramparts. There is plenty of circumstantial evidence that Cadbury was indeed Camelot, but sadly no solid proof.

In folklore, however, King Arthur and his knights are said to lie sleeping inside the hill, awaiting the time when they will be called to help England in her hour of need. On **Midsummer** Eve every seven years, Arthur leads his men out on horseback, and they go for water to a spring by the church at Sutton Montis.

Location: 8 kilometres (5 miles) W of Wincanton, Somerset; footpath near South Cadbury church leads into fort. OS ref: ST 627250.

Spiral

The spiral symbolizes growth and development, cosmic forms in motion. Carvings of spirals can sometimes be found on stones at **prehistoric sites**, where they are believed to mark special astronomical events. (*See, for example,* **Long Meg and Her Daughters.**) **Dragons** left spiral coils on the hills they encircled; the dragon or **serpent** guarded **treasure** at the heart of the spiral **maze**.

Spirit lines

In the folklore of many countries, including Britain, corpses were carried along an ancient straight road to the cemetery. Linear prehistoric structures, such as the **cursus** and stone rows, may also have been associated with death rituals, linked with the belief that the spirits of the dead travelled in straight lines. Further links are seen with the **ley** theory of aligned ancient sites, and with the Chinese practice of **feng-shui**. Further discussion of spirit ways and ghost roads can be found in Paul Devereux's book *Symbolic Landscapes*. Devereux describes landscape lines as 'the symbolic representations of shamanic spirit journey routes:

flight paths of the soul symbolically transferred to the solid earth.'

Standing stones

A **megalith** or **menhir** erected usually in prehistoric times, either singly (e.g. **Rudston monolith**) or in circles (*see* **Stone circle**) or in rows. They varied in size from huge (e.g. **Stonehenge**) to tiny (e.g. **Hill o' Many Stanes**), and although they usually stood upright, they were occasionally laid flat (as at **Arbor Low**). It is certain that their functions too were many, among them being to commemorate an important person (in the same way that we erect memorials today); to delineate a ritual enclosure (obviously a very important site, if wooden stakes were not considered suitable although much easier to obtain and position); and to act as markers for astronomical observations (*see* **Astronomy**). They may also have had more symbolic functions: the tall, upright stones might have been phallic symbols (*see* **Phallus**), especially when in close conjunction with a diamond-shaped stone or a circular **holed stone** or stone circle, all of which are thought to have symbolized the female. Good examples of male and female stones together include the **Men-an-Tol**, **Avebury**, the **Hurlers**.

Various legends explained why standing stones were erected and how they behaved. See, for example, **Cock-crow stones**, **Countless stones**, **Devil's Arrows**, **Female stones**, **Moving stones**, **Petrifaction**, **Rollright Stones**, **Trellech**.

Stone Age

See **Neolithic**

Stone circles

Although more than 900 stone circles have been located in Britain, the reason why they were built is still not known. Many are now unimpressive, with only one or two small random stones still surviving, but some are well preserved and situated in breathtaking locations, as at **Castlerigg** in Cumbria. The circles were built over a period of about 1,800 years from 3000 to 1200 BC – roughly the length of time that Christianity has been in existence. Just as Christian churches vary in shape and size, so too do stone circles. They were not all circular, for example, a fact discovered by Professor Alexander Thom who surveyed them over several decades and found egg shapes, ellipses, and flattened circles, all involving geometrical precision. Sometimes several circles were erected together, as at **The Hurlers** in Cornwall, where there are three; or a circle was part of a more complex design, as at **Callanish** where the circle has leading from it a stone avenue and stone rows, the whole forming a cross shape.

It seems likely that stone circles were used for what we would now call scientific or religious purposes, or maybe a mixture of both. They may have been intended as early scientific instruments, and could have been used to make astronomical calculations. (*See* **Astronomy**.) On a more day-to-day level, it is probable that rituals and ceremonies were also performed at stone circles, though we can only guess at the intention behind such ceremonies. Perhaps the people hoped to promote **fertility** in the earth and in themselves, perhaps they hoped to communicate with the gods or spirits that they worshipped. (*See also* **Circles**.)

Stonehenge

Possibly the most famous **prehistoric site** in the world, Stonehenge is in many ways Britain's most impressive antiquity – though at present the atmosphere tends to be spoilt by the sheer number of visitors who are usually there, and the fact that the site is insensitively presented, with too much concrete, too many fences, and a main road passing close by. Older people remember that not so long ago it was possible to park by the road and just wander into the stones – and have them all to yourself. But there are plans afoot for major changes which should help to re-establish the importance of this major site; though for the present it is best visited early in the day and out of the tourist season.

There are a number of books devoted solely to Stonehenge which describe its archaeological features in detail. Here we will concentrate on some of the beliefs and theories that have been published. According to folklore, it was called Giants' Dance, probably from the belief that the stones were petrified **giants**. It was also believed that the stones had been erected by **Merlin**, King Arthur's magician, being brought from Ireland (and previously fetched from Africa by giants). The stones were believed to have **healing** powers, and water that had been poured over the stones was then used to bathe the sick. Stonehenge has been seen as a **Druid** temple, though this is unlikely as it was in existence 2,000 years before the Druids were active, and their temples were groves of trees rather than stone structures. During this century, some scientists have interpreted Stonehenge as an astronomical observatory where priest-astronomers practised an early form of **astronomy**, perhaps in order to predict the behaviour of the sky gods.

Stonehenge has also been seen as a place rich in sexual imagery: there are the phallic bluestones (*see* **Phallus**) and the female trilithons – two upright stones capped by a third to form a classic female receptive symbol. The layout of the stones also lends itself to a sexual interpretation. Although the decay of the centuries has resulted in fallen stones and an opening-out of the monument, when it was complete the circles of trilithons and inner bluestones would have given an enclosed feeling to the interior of the site, and it has been suggested that this symbolized the womb. Its opening pointed towards the phallic Heel Stone, and at **midsummer** sunrise the shadow of this stone penetrates into the centre of the womb, the only time of the year when this happens. G.T. Meaden has developed the sexual theory in his book *The Stonehenge Solution*, where he describes the 'Marriage of the Gods' in great detail.

Despite all the excavations, all the legends, and all the theories, the true purpose behind the original erection and later developments of this amazing structure, with its 45-ton stones and evidence of the skilful workmanship of 4-5000 years ago, remains shrouded in mystery.

Location: 3 kilometres (2 miles) W of Amesbury, Wiltshire. OS ref: SU 123422.

Storms

To disturb an ancient site was to invite disaster, and there are many stories telling how storms broke out whenever anyone began to dig for **treasure** in a burial mound. Treasure is said to be hidden in the **hillfort** on top of the hill Moel Arthur in the Clwydian range (Clwyd), its exact position marked by lights, but as soon as anyone begins to dig for it, they are frightened away by terrible storms. In his *Survey of Cornwall* published in 1602 Richard Carew tells how an attempt to find treasure under a stone near Fowey ended in the men seeking shelter from a storm:

'in a faire Moone-shine night [the men went to seek treasure]: a working they fall, their labour shortneth, their hope increaseth, a pot of Gold is the least of their expectation . . .

In midst of their toyling the skie gathereth clouds, the Moone-light is ouercast with darknesse, downe fals a mightie showre, up riseth a blustering tempest, the thunder cracketh, the lightning flasheth: in conclusion our money-seekers . . . are forced to abandon their enterprise and seeke shelter of the next house they could get into.'

Even in more recent times similar events have occurred when archaeologists have been excavating sites.

People interfering with sacred sites have also experienced other problems, including illness, death, and poltergeist outbreaks. Details of such occurrences are given in our book *The Secret Country*.

Sun

The sun and the moon are symbols of the active and the passive principles of the Universe, similar to the relationship between heaven and earth: the sky symbolizes activity (male) and the earth symbolizes passivity (female). In its behaviour the moon is passive in that it merely reflects the light radiated by the sun. The sun was the bringer of light, warmth, and **fertility**; the moon, being cold, was connected with death. Many **prehistoric sites** show that their builders were aware of the movements of the sun and the moon. A major part of early **astronomy** was probably dedicated to plotting the movements of both sun and moon, and it is likely that certain stone monuments were used to achieve this. Archaeologists have reported very many instances of links between the orientation of sites and stones and the movements of sun and moon, but it is difficult to do other than guess at the precise use made of the information obtained. (*See also* **Maes Howe passage grave**.)

T

Terrestrial zodiacs
See **Glastonbury Zodiac**

Tintagel
There is hardly a more dramatic location in Britain than the site of Tintagel Castle in Cornwall. The village of Tintagel is very touristy, especially in high summer, but a short walk away are the cliff-top ruins of a 12th-century castle, among which are also to be found some Celtic remains. Tintagel Castle is best known, of course, as the site of King **Arthur's** birth, though in reality this' fact' is highly debatable. According to the legend, it was the magician **Merlin** who was responsible: he engineered the union of Ygraine, wife of Gorlois, Duke of Cornwall, with Uther Pendragon, High King of Britain, and the result was the birth of Arthur. In a version of the story by the poet Tennyson, the baby Arthur was lifted from the sea by Merlin, and the cave where this happened can still be visited. It is known as Merlin's Cave, and is said to be haunted by him. Other things to look out for at Tintagel, connected with the legend, are the rock features known as Arthur's Footprint, Arthur's Chair, and Arthur's Cups and Saucers (*see also* **Footprints**).
Location: On the north Cornish coast, 22.5 kilometres (14 miles) N of Bodmin. OS ref: SX 048891.

Tor
See **Glastonbury**

Tracks
Alfred Watkins saw **leys** as 'old straight tracks' – his classic book on the subject is called *The Old Straight Track* – simply the remains of prehistoric trackways. Ancient roads do still exist, and some of them do follow the course of leys, but many decades of research

has found that the answer is not so simple. (*See also* **Spirit lines**.)

Treasure

Not surprisingly, there are traditions of buried treasure at numerous **prehistoric sites**, especially **barrows** and burial mounds, and sometimes these have been proved to be correct. In Clwyd, for example, it was said that the ghost of a huge man dressed in gold haunted a barrow called Bryn yr Ellyllon (Hill of the Goblins) at Mold, and when it was opened during the last century, a gold corselet or cape was found inside. In some instances, it was said that people who tried digging for buried treasure were frightened away by tremendous **storms**, as at **Trencrom Hill** in Cornwall. **Caves** full of treasure were also widely rumoured. The treasure in King Arthur's Cave near the River Wye in Herefordshire was hidden there by King **Arthur** when he was being chased by his enemies, and **Merlin** put a spell on the cave so that the treasure couldn't be found. One man actually found treasure in a cave near Ogwen Lake in Gwynedd, but he couldn't lift it to take it away. So he decided to mark the cave and come back with a friend. He left a trail of chips cut off his walking stick – but when he returned they had all disappeared. Fairy treasure is only illusory. A harper walking home late one night after playing for a party, was passing Llyn dau Ychain on the moors above Cerrigydrudion in Clwyd when he came across a brightly lit palace and was invited inside. He played for the dancers, and was paid with gold and silver coins. At dawn, everyone left and he lay on a couch to rest – but when he awoke at noon, he was lying on a pile of heather and the coins in his hat were dead leaves. Many more stories of hidden treasure can be found in our books *The Enchanted Land* and *The Secret Country*.

Trees

The sacred nature of the tree shows itself in many ways: it is the centre of the world and supports the universe: it is a symbol of life, of inexhaustible **fertility**, of immortality, and of rebirth. There is much evidence from all over Britain to show how important trees have always been to man, and not only in the most obvious ways of providing fuel and materials. Special trees were decorated annually, and some still are: at Appleton in Cheshire the **custom** of Bawming (adorning) the Thorn is still carried out on or around Old **Midsummer** Day (5 July), using flowers and ribbons, and children dance round the tree. At Aston-on-Clun in Shropshire, 29 May is Arbor Day when flags on poles are hung in a black poplar tree, and left there till the next year. A pageant is also held, with maypole and morris dancing underneath the tree. Dancing around trees may have been a form of tree-worship, closely paralleled in the custom of dancing round the maypole on **May Day**. The maypole was originally a tree fetched specially from the woods, and it has a phallic symbolism (*see* **Phallus**).

Different species of trees have been venerated, such as the thorn. The attention paid to the Holy Thorn at **Glastonbury** is all that remains of an English thorn cult: until quite recently, people would gather on Old Christmas Eve (5 January) to watch the Holy Thorns flower (there were bushes in Somerset, Herefordshire and elsewhere, as well as at Glastonbury). We have already mentioned the custom of Bawming the Thorn; thorn trees were often sited close to **holy wells** and used as 'rag bushes' where pilgrims visiting the wells would leave a piece of cloth as part of the **healing** ritual. There was a Well of the Thorn Tree at Kirk Malew on the Isle of Man. Other species of trees were also found at holy wells, including yew and ash. The association between holy wells and sacred trees goes back many centuries, as indicated by the contents of a **Celtic** shaft-well discovered at Ashill in Norfolk. Formed of wood and 12 metres (40 feet) deep, it was found to contain pottery, bones, a basket and a knife, and, below 6 metres (20 feet), layers of urns embedded in the leaves and nuts of the hazel tree. Since Celtic times, and maybe also before, the hazel tree has been a holy tree with fertility associations, and even in recent times country people still connected it with love and childbirth.

The fertility symbolism of the tree takes several forms. In one aspect it is a phallic symbol, jutting out of the earth; in another aspect it is female, bearing fruit and rounded in shape. In some parts of the world, resin from coniferous trees was regarded as the **Earth Mother's** menstruation, which reminds us of British legends concerning bleeding yew, elder and hawthorn trees. The most famous 'bleeding' yew is in **Nevern** churchyard, Dyfed: we have seen the red liquid oozing from its trunk. It was life-blood rather than menstrual blood which flowed from a holy thorn being cut down at Clehonger in Herefordshire, or so the story goes. The man committing the evil act was so terrified when he saw the blood coming from its trunk that he left the thorn where it was. Bleeding elders are usually witches in disguise, like the famous tree near the

Rollright Stones in Oxfordshire. A witch turned a king and his army into **standing stones**, and she herself became an elder tree. When the tree was cut during the annual Midsummer Eve ceremonies, it bled.

There are also fertility themes connected with trees, and some special trees were visited by those hoping for love and marriage. For one example from many, the Trysting Pine (or Kissing or Wishing Tree) on Barnham Cross Common near Thetford in Norfolk has acquired magical powers because its trunk has formed into a loop, and the ritual is either to pull off a cone, hold it in the right hand, put your head through the loop and make a wish, or, for couples visiting the tree, to hold hands and kiss through the loop. Couples would sometimes be married beneath a sacred tree known as a Marriage Oak. A bride often included myrtle in her bouquet, for it was considered to be lucky, and would bring fertility. There was also a marriage-divination ritual involving myrtle. Later, orange-blossom took over from myrtle; and nuts were also often included somewhere in the marriage festivities, being symbols of fertility. A good nut harvest signified plenty of babies during the coming year, with double nuts meaning twins. A girl should not go nutting on a Sunday, for she would meet the **Devil** and have a baby before her wedding!

The promotion of fertility was intended by the widespread use of trees and foliage in May Day celebrations throughout Europe. In the belief that the tree-spirit would fertilize women and cattle, and make the crops grow, houses and farm buildings were decked with greenery, while whole trees were cut and then re-erected in the village. Although later a pole was left permanently erected and then decorated at each year's May festivities, originally a new tree was brought each year. It was a phallic symbol, suggesting the flow of **energy** between cosmos and earth which the people were seeking to invoke.

Even in the 20th century people still revere trees. In the 1930s when the road at Temple by Loch Ness needed widening, no Scot could be found who would cut down a certain tree because it was said to be the tree under which St Ninian sat, and an Englishman had to be brought in to cut it down. In November 1991 the first National Tree Dressing Day was held, staged by the arts, conservation and environmental awareness group Common Ground, as a way of reminding people of the importance of trees to the health of the planet.

Trellech

Three separate antiquities in this small Welsh village are all worth exploring. The major feature consists of three tall **standing stones** known as Harold's Stones. There are at least three stories explaining their origin. One tells how they were thrown here by a local **giant** called Jack o' Kent. He jumped from one mountain, the Sugar Loaf, to another, the Skirrid, where he played quoits with the stones, tossing them to Trellech. Or he was at Beacon Hill, engaged in a throwing match with the **Devil**. No one is quite sure about the true identity of Jack o' Kent. He might have been based upon John Kent, an astrologer and writer on **witchcraft** in the 15th century. Stories about Jack were widespread in this area: he was said to have made a pact with the Devil, besting him in numerous trials of strength.

The standing stones are today known as the Harold Stones because another story claims they are a memorial to a battle in the 11th century in which the Welsh were beaten by the English led by King Harold Godwinson. All who fell in the battle are said to be buried in a huge mound called Tump Terret, which stands in a farmyard in the village, reached by a footpath. In the village church not far away is a 17th-century sundial carved with the three antiquities – the stones, the mound, and also the **holy well** which can be found just outside the village.

Called St Anne's Well or Virtuous Well, it is protected by an old stone building. Steps lead down to a pool where the well water collects. There were once nine wells at Trellech, according to tradition, and each cured a different disease. They were very popular in earlier centuries, and were said to cure 'the scurvy, colic and other distempers'. St Anne's Well is also a wishing well: you just drop a pebble into the water and a plentiful uprush of bubbles signifies that the wish has been granted. A few bubbles means a delay, and none means the wish has failed. **Fairies** were said to dance at the wells on **Midsummer** Eve, and to drink water from harebells, which would be found strewn around the next morning. Once, when a farmer closed the wells, a 'little old man' appeared and told him that, as a punishment, no water would flow on his farm. He quickly reopened the wells and his supply returned.

In most areas of Britain, tales of **underground passages** are found in the local folklore, and at Trellech it is said that the nuns from Tintern Abbey three miles away would travel through a tunnel to bathe in the medicinal pool (presumably St Anne's Well).

Alas, no such tunnel has been found, and there never were nuns at Tintern Abbey! Another legend tells of music heard underground below a meadow at Trellech. The ground was excavated to reveal a cave in which two old men were playing harp and violin. They said they had been there for many years, taking turns to venture out for food; they died shortly after being discovered.

Location: Trellech is about 9.5 kilometres (6 miles) S of Monmouth, Gwent. Harold's Stones OS ref: SO 499051.

Trencrom Hill

The tumbled stones around the top of the hill are the remains of an **Iron Age hillfort**; but in folklore this was a **giant's** dwelling, and one of those who lived here was the Giant of Trecrobben, who was also involved in the activities on St Michael's Mount. The giants enjoyed playing bowls, and one of their 'woods', called the Bowl Rock, can be found at the bottom of the hill where it was left after it rolled down. The giants hid their **treasure** in the hill, and it was guarded by spriggans, who were a sort of cross between giants and **fairies**. They were incredibly ugly, and as well as guarding treasure they used to steal children, leaving their own ugly ones behind. They would also bring bad weather to damage the crops, and make whirlwinds in the cornfields (were they also responsible for **crop circles**, perhaps?). One folklorist claimed they were the ghosts of old giants, and although usually small, they could swell to an enormous size if they needed to. A foolhardy man who started digging on Trencrom Hill, in search of the treasure, was frightened away by a **storm** and by the appearance of the spriggans, who were growing larger as they came nearer, and who looked 'as ugly as if they would eat him'.

Location: 5 kilometres (3 miles) S of St Ives, Cornwall. OS ref: SW 518362.

Trethevy Quoit

An impressive example of a **dolmen**, standing almost 4.5 metres (15 feet) high, with a 3.5-metre (12-foot) capstone supported on seven uprights. The capstone has a small hole in it, the purpose of which is unknown. The front upright also has a hole cut from its lower right-hand side, perhaps to enable bodies to be placed inside the tomb (assuming that that was its use). The whole structure was probably at least partly covered with earth when first built. Granite was used, which has a high natural radiation count; this rock may have been chosen with a purpose (*see* **Quartz**).

Location: 5 kilometres (3 miles) N of Liskeard, Cornwall. OS ref: SX 259688.

Tumulus

An alternative name for a **barrow**.

U

Uffington White Horse

First recorded in the 12th century, the Uffington White Horse is probably Britain's oldest **hill figure**. Although it is very difficult to date these figures accurately, in 1995 a procedure called optical stimulated luminescence dating (known more simply as optical dating) was used and this has given a date of 1400 to 600 BC, which means that the horse was first created in the late **Bronze Age** 3,000 years ago, which is 1,000 years earlier than had previously been believed. The stylized figure is like **horses** seen on Celtic **Iron Age** coins of 2,000 years ago, although in actual fact it scarcely resembles a horse, and indeed could just as easily be seen as a cat!

Folklore has identified him as a **dragon**, and has also given the name Dragon Hill to a strange flat-topped hill in the deep valley below the figure. There is a gleaming white bare patch on the hilltop: this is said to be the place where St George slew the dragon, and where its blood fell no grass will grow. The horse or dragon is an amazing 111 metres (121 yards) long, and is only properly visible from the air. A path leads across the top of the hill to his head, so that you can stand above him and look down at Dragon Hill, and at the valley known as the Manger, where it was once the custom to roll cheeses downhill. This happened along with other festivities and sports, eating and drinking, which took place every seventh year when people gathered to clean or 'scour' the horse. Chalk figures are soon overgrown and lost if not scoured regularly, which is why in recent years their outlines have usually been made more permanent.

On the hilltop above the horse is Uffington Castle, an Iron Age **hillfort** with bank and ditch, and not far away is the ancient trackway known as The Ridgeway. A **ley** passes through Uffington Castle and Dragon Hill; full details can be found in Paul Devereux's book *The New Ley Hunter's Guide*.

Location: Above Uffington village in the Vale of the White Horse, between Swindon and Wantage, Oxfordshire. OS ref: SU 302866.

UFOs

Unidentified flying objects (or flying saucers, as they were originally known) are still a mystery, despite 50 years of research and investigation. Some people are sure that they are craft from other planets in our solar system or beyond, bringing alien visitors; other people are equally sure that they are nothing but a modern myth, and that all the sightings are either hoaxes or misidentifications of natural or man-made phenomena. Leaving aside the question as to whether any UFOs are alien craft, what is certain is that many sightings are not of objects at all, but simply of strange lights. These could have many explanations, from stars and planets, to aircraft and laser shows. But some could be manifestations of little-known and even less understood phenomena such as ball lightning and **earth lights**.

Underground passages

If we are to believe folklore, there are many underground passages criss-crossing the landscape. In fact, few of them have been shown to exist. The stories told often include hidden **treasure** and **ghosts**, as well as ill-fated musicians. One passage was said to run several miles from Castell Coch (the Red Castle) to Cardiff Castle in South Wales: in a **cave** under Castell Coch was an iron chest filled with treasure which belonged to Ivor the Little. Three huge eagles are chained to the chest to guard it, and no one has been able to outwit them and steal the treasure. Other birds (cockerels, ravens, crows) guard other treasure chests; sometimes snakes are the guardians. Several passages, such as that said to link Binham Priory to Walsingham Abbey in Norfolk, are reputed to be where fiddlers have disappeared. In an attempt to find out where a passage led, a fiddler would follow it while playing his instrument, and someone would follow the sound of the music above ground. But the music would stop halfway along, at a small wood now called Fiddler's Copse, and the musician would never been seen again.

Tales of underground passages are so widespread, often in places where no physical passage could be constructed, that we begin to wonder if the straight line represented by the passage may not in fact represent something else, perhaps a **ley** (alignment of ancient sites) or a **spirit line**.

Up-Helly-Aa

A pagan fire festival held in the Shetland Isles annually at the end of January, marking the end of the Yule (**Christmas**) festivities. Until 100 years ago, the main feature was the dragging of blazing tar-barrels through the streets of Lerwick, but this was eventually banned because it was too dangerous, and now the event features a torchlight procession and a burning ship (a large model Norse galley). There are also Guizers, men in costume, whose role was once to bring luck to houses and their occupants. They now attend to the burning of the galley, before performing entertainment through the night. (*See also* **Fire ceremonies**.)

W

Water

It may be self-evident that water is a source of life and growth, and without it the land, the crops, the animals and mankind will perish. But symbolically water can also be seen as a potent fertilizing liquid, so that the scattering of water in some traditional **customs** does not necessarily imply a charm for the procurement of rain, but may be used to bring 'good luck' or fecundity to those upon whom it falls. In many parts of Britain there was keen competition on New Year's morning to be the first to draw water from wells, ponds or streams. This water was called the 'Flower' or 'Cream' of the well and would bring the drawer 'good luck' for the coming year. In Scotland it was given to cows to drink to increase their milk yield, and in Herefordshire a farm servant would present it to her mistress in return for a gift of money. If it was kept in the house it would protect the household during the coming year, but an unmarried girl would keep it herself and would expect to be married during the next 12 months. In Scotland the 'Cream of the Well' was brought into the house in silence, a little was drunk by each person, and every room and byre was sprinkled with it.

Water sprinkling was also practised at New Year, principally in South Wales. Early in the morning of New Year's Day, youths would visit local houses carrying a vessel of fresh spring water and evergreen twigs, which they would use to sprinkle water on anyone they met, and on the rooms of the houses they visited. Recently married couples would be liberally sprinkled as they lay in bed; and mothers would sprinkle the faces of their sleeping children. (For more on the importance of water, *see* **Holy wells**.)

Well-dressing

Water has always been venerated, especially at springs and **holy wells**, and one of the rituals which has survived to the present day (though not uninterruptedly) is well-dressing. Originally garlands were used, but the decoration became more elaborate so that now pictures of religious subjects are constructed from natural objects like flower-petals, seeds, berries, leaves, bark, and moss, all pressed into soft clay. The best place to see dressed wells is Derbyshire, where many villages celebrate in this way in spring and summer, but the custom is now spreading to other parts of the country.

Wells
See **Holy wells**

West Kennet Long Barrow

This fine **megalithic** tomb is one of the earliest structures still surviving in Britain, dating from the **Neolithic** era up to 6,000 years ago. The 97-metre (320-foot) long earth mound contains a 10-metre (33-foot) stone passage with side chambers, this being used as a **burial chamber** with remains of burials being found during archaeological excavations. But it is unlikely that the **barrow** was used solely for burials: most likely rituals and ceremonies were performed there also, perhaps connected with death and the after-life. There is evidence that the structure was in use for as long as 1,000 years, and in some ways its use parallels that of our historic churches and cathedrals. When it was no longer useful, it was filled up with chalk rubble and boulders, and three huge stone slabs were used to seal the entrance. Now the interior has been cleared out, and can be entered. At sunrise on **Midsummer** Day, it is traditionally visited by a ghostly priest with a large white dog.

Location: 8 kilometres (5 miles) W of Marlborough, Wiltshire; not far from **Silbury Hill** and **Avebury**; reached by footpath across field from A4 road. OS ref: SU 105677.

Whispering Knights
See **Moving stones; Rollright Stones**

Wishing stones and wells

Some stones were believed to be lucky, and able to grant wishes. Young people who wanted to find a sweetheart would walk nine times round the Wishing Post, a pillar in the dungeon of Oystermouth Castle on the Gower (West Glamorgan), while making their wish. There was also a Wishing Stone among Brimham Rocks (North Yorkshire): you had to place your right-hand middle finger in the hole and wish. These are only two examples of many such stones countrywide. **Holy wells** believed to have the power to grant wishes were also common, and again certain rituals had to be followed. At Walsingham (Norfolk), the wishing wells are in two small stone basins. The wish-maker had to place his right knee in a stone between the wells, dip I is bare hands into the water up to the wrists, make a silent wish, then withdraw his hands and swallow the water held in them. People still throw coins into wells and hope to be granted some good luck.

Witchcraft

Witches have traditionally used **prehistoric sites**, especially **stone circles**, as places to meet and perform their ceremonies and rituals. One of these meeting places was Witches' Rock near Zennor (Cornwall) where all the local witches were said to meet on **Midsummer** Eve. Perhaps the best-known witchcraft location in Britain was Pendle Hill and the Forest of Pendle in Lancashire. Several women from this area were tried for witchcraft in the 1600s, and eight were hanged. Details of their confessions were published in *A Wonderfulle Discoverie of Witches in the County of Lancaster* by Thomas Potts, but it is probable that much of the evidence against them was fabricated, and that torture was applied to make them confess. There are still reminders of Pendle's past fame as a hotbed of witchcraft to be found at Newchurch-in-Pendle. Alice Nutter, one of the alleged witches, is buried there, and a stone and slate eye can be seen on the church tower, put there to protect the congregation against the witches' evil eye.

One of the witches' claimed skills was to be able to create storms, and in a Scottish witch trial in 1662 a witch confessed that she and her associates used to do this at a **standing stone** known as the Kempock Stane overlooking the Clyde Estuary (Renfrew):

> When we raise the wind we take a rag of cloth and wet it in water, and we take a beetle [mallet] and knock the rag on a stone and we say thrice over –
> > I knock this rag upon this stane,
> > To raise the wind in the devil's name.
> > It shall not lie until I please again.

The witches may have used the stone in this way because it was generally believed to have power over the weather. Fishermen would bring gifts and baskets of sand from the seashore, and they would circle the stone, sprinkling sand and asking for good weather, calm seas and a large catch (*see* **Offerings**). One of the witches claimed to have danced around the Kempock Stane with the **Devil**, and they had intended to throw it into the sea to create bad luck for the fishermen.

The dances the witches performed at stone circles could have been intended to raise **energy** which would be added to the natural earth energy already at the site, and they may have been able to direct energy to bring about a successful outcome to their rituals.

Witches have other links with ancient sites, for example at the **Rollright Stones** where a witch turned into an elder tree that bled when cut, after she had caused a king and his soldiers to be turned to stone. The **stone circle** and **standing stone** known as **Long Meg and Her Daughters** were said to be a coven of witches turned to stone by a magician (*see* **Petrifaction**). Sometimes witches were responsible for changing the location of a **church**, for example at Wendover in Buckinghamshire, where the stones from the original site nearer to the town were carried to the present site by witches.

Wrekin, The

This prominent hill in Shropshire has always been a special place. Chosen for the site of a fortress in the **Iron Age**, its very presence was accounted for by tales of **giants**. In one story, a giant with a grudge against Shrewsbury was carrying a load of earth with which to bury the town. He met a cobbler on the road and asked him the way. Realizing what the giant intended to do, the cobbler showed him the bag of boots he was carrying and told him that he had worn them all out since leaving Shrewsbury. Disheartened by the long journey apparently still ahead of him, the giant dumped his load of earth, forming the Wrekin. The soil he scraped from his boots formed the neighbouring Ercall Hill.

In another story, two giants built the Wrekin as a safe place to live, using earth they dug from the bed of the nearby River Severn. Traces of their presence can still be seen: bare patches on the hill are said to be their **footprints**; while the Needle's Eye, a cleft rock on the summit, was formed as the result of a quarrel between the two giants. One hit out at the other with his spade, missed, and split the rock. The attacking giant was himself attacked by the other's pet raven, which pecked out his eyes. The tears he shed fell into a rock basin, now called the Raven's Bowl, still to be seen on the summit and supposedly always full of water. The blinded giant was overpowered by his former friend and imprisoned in Ercall Hill, from where his groans can still be heard at dead of night.

The Raven's Bowl was also known as the Cuckoo's Cup, and in another tale was said to have been miraculously formed as a drinking place for those birds. There was a **holy well** on the hill, named for St Hawthorn, and its water was supposed to be effective in curing skin diseases. The Gates of Heaven and Hell were also to be found on the Wrekin – they were the names given to openings in the banks of the Iron Age **hillfort**. So much folklore devoted to this hill shows that it was thought to be a special place with otherworldly associations. The Wrekin is still a magical place today, somehow set apart from the 20th-century scene that now surrounds it.

Location: 13 kilometres (8 miles) SE of Shrewsbury, Shropshire. OS ref: SJ 625080.

Y

Yule log
  See **Christmas; Customs; Fire ceremonies; Sacrifice**

Z

Zodiac
   See **Glastonbury Zodiac**

Sacred and Mysterious Places to Visit

There are so many special places in Britain that it would be impossible to list them all. Here is a small selection; they are described in more detail in the body of the dictionary. Many more places to visit can be found in our other books (*see Bibliography*), especially *A Guide to Ancient Sites in Britain*, *Ancient Mysteries of Britain*, *Atlas of Magical Britain* and *The Enchanted Land*.

Arbor Low, Derbyshire
Avebury, Wiltshire
Bath, Avon
Cairnholy chambered cairns, Kirkcudbright
Callanish, Isle of Lewis
Carn Euny settlement and fogou, Cornwall
Castlerigg stone circle, Cumbria
Cerne Abbas Giant, Dorset
Chalice Well, Somerset
Clava cairns, Inverness
Coventina's Well, Northumberland
Llyn Cynwch, Gwynedd
Devil's Arrows, North Yorkshire
Dinas Bran, Clwyd
Dinas Emrys, Gwynedd
Dunadd, Argyll
Eildon Hills, Roxburgh
Fairy Hill, Perth
Glastonbury, Somerset
Gop Cairn, Clwyd
Herefordshire Beacon, Hereford & Worcester

Hill o' Many Stanes, Caithness
The Hurlers stone circles, Cornwall
Jarlshof, Shetland
Kilmartin cairn cemetery, Argyll
Kilpeck church, Hereford
Knowlton Circles, Dorset
Lanyon Quoit, Cornwall
Lindisfarne, Northumberland
Llanddwyn Island, Gwynedd
Long Man of Wilmington, East Sussex
Long Meg and Her Daughters, Cumbria
Maes Howe passage grave, Orkney
Maiden Castle, Dorset
Men-an-Tol, Cornwall
Merry Maidens, Cornwall
Mitchell's Fold stone circle, Shropshire
Mousa broch, Shetland
Nevern, Dyfed
Old Sarum, Wiltshire
Pentre Ifan, Dyfed

123

Preseli Hills, Dyfed
Rollright Stones, Oxfordshire
Rudston monolith, Humberside
St Cybi's Well, Gwynedd
St Govan's Chapel, Dyfed
St Keyne's Well, Cornwall
St Non's Well, Dyfed
St Winefride's Well, Clwyd
Silbury Hill, Wiltshire
Skara Brae, Orkney
South Cadbury Castle, Somerset

Stonehenge, Wiltshire
Tintagel, Cornwall
Trellech, Gwent
Trencrom Hill, Cornwall
Trethevy Quoit, Cornwall
Uffington White Horse,
Oxfordshire
West Kennet Long Barrow,
Wiltshire
The Wrekin, Shropshire

Bibliography

Alexander, Marc, *British Folklore, Myths and Legends*, Weidenfeld & Nicolson, 1982

Andersen, Jørgen, *The Witch on the Wall: Medieval Erotic Sculpture in the British Isles*, George Allen & Unwin, 1977

Anderson, William, *Green Man: The Archetype of our Oneness with the Earth*, HarperCollins Publishers, 1990

Ashe, Geoffrey, *Camelot and the Vision of Albion*, William Heinemann, 1971

—— *A Guidebook to Arthurian Britain*, Longman, 1980

—— *Mythology of the British Isles*, Methuen London, 1990

Barber, Chris, & John Godfrey Williams, *The Ancient Stones of Wales*, Blorenge Books, 1989

Barber, Chris, & David Pykitt, *Journey to Avalon: The Final Discovery of King Arthur*, Blorenge Books, 1993

Beckensall, Stan, *Rock Carvings of Northern Britain*, Shire Publications, 1986

Begg, Ean & Deike Rich, *On the Trail of Merlin: A Guide to the Celtic Mystery Tradition*, Aquarian Press, 1991

Bewley, Robert, *English Heritage Book of Prehistoric Settlements*, B. T. Batsford, 1994

Bord, Janet, *Mazes and Labyrinths of the World*, Latimer New Dimensions, 1976

Bord, Janet & Colin, *Mysterious Britain*, Garnstone Press, 1972; Thorsons, 1995

—— *The Secret Country: An Interpretation of the Folklore of Ancient Sites in the British Isles*, Paul Elek, 1976; Paladin Books, 1978

—— *A Guide to Ancient Sites in Britain*, Latimer New Dimensions, 1978; Paladin Books, 1979

—— *Alien Animals: A Worldwide Investigation*, Granada Publishing, 1980

—— *Earth Rites: Fertility Practices in Pre-industrial Britain*, Granada Publishing, 1982

—— *Sacred Waters: Holy Wells and Water Lore in Britain and Ireland*, Granada Publishing, 1985

—— *Ancient Mysteries of Britain*, Grafton Books, 1986; Paladin Books, 1987

—— *Modern Mysteries of Britain: One Hundred Years of Strange Events*, Grafton Books, 1987

—— *Atlas of Magical Britain*, Sidgwick & Jackson, 1990

—— *The Enchanted Land: Myths and Legends of Britain's Landscape*, Thorsons, 1995

Broadhurst, Paul, *Secret Shrines: In Search of the old Holy Wells of Cornwall*, Paul Broadhurst, 1988

—— *Tintagel and the Arthurian Mythos*, Pendragon Press, 1992

Burl, Aubrey, *The Stone Circles of the British Isles*, Yale University Press, 1976

—— *Prehistoric Avebury*, Yale University Press, 1979

—— *Rites of the Gods*, J.M. Dent & Sons Ltd, 1981

—— *Prehistoric Astronomy and Ritual*, Shire Publications, 1983

—— *The Stonehenge People*, J.M. Dent, 1987

—— *From Carnac to Callanish: The Prehistoric Stone Rows and Avenues of Britain, Ireland and Brittany*, Yale University Press, 1993

—— *Stone Circles: A Guide to the Megalithic Rings of Britain, Ireland and Brittany*, Yale University Press, 1995

Castleden, Rodney, *The Wilmington Giant: The Quest for a Lost Myth*, Turnstone Press, 1983

Cavendish, Richard, *King Arthur and the Grail: The Arthurian Legends and their Meaning*, Weidenfeld and Nicolson, 1978

Chetan, Anand, and Diana Brueton, *The Sacred Yew*, Arkana, 1994

Chippindale, Christopher, *Stonehenge Complete*, Thames and Hudson, first published 1983, revised edition 1994

Clarke, David, *A Guide to Britain's Pagan Heritage*, Robert Hale, 1995

Coghlan, Ronan, *The Illustrated Encyclopaedia of Arthurian Legends*, Element Books, 1993

Cunliffe, Barry, *English Heritage Book of Iron Age Britain*, B.T. Batsford, 1995

Dames, Michael, *The Silbury Treasure: The Great Goddess Rediscovered*, Thames and Hudson, 1976

—— *The Avebury Cycle*, Thames and Hudson, 1977

Darrah, John, *The Real Camelot: Paganism and the Arthurian Romances*, Thames and Hudson, 1981

Davidson, Hilda Ellis, *The Lost Beliefs of Northern Europe*, Routledge, 1993

Devereux, Paul, *Earth Lights*: *Towards an Explanation of the UFO Enigma*, Turnstone Press, 1982

—— *Earth Lights Revelation*: *UFOs and Mystery Lightform Phenomena*: *The Earth's Secret Energy Force*, Blandford Press, 1989

—— & John Steel, David Kubrin, *Earthmind*: *A Modern Adventure in Ancient Wisdom*, Harper & Row, 1989

—— *Places of Power*: *Secret Energies at Ancient Sites*: *A Guide to Observed or measured Phenomena*, Blandford Press, 1990

—— *Earth Memory*: *The Holistic Earth Mysteries Approach to Decoding Ancient Sacred Sites*, Quantum, 1991

—— & Laurence Main, *The Old Straight Tracks of Wessex*, Thornhill Press, 1992

—— *Secrets of Ancient and Sacred Places*, Blandford Press, 1992

—— *Symbolic Landscapes*: *The Dreamtime Earth and Avebury's Open Secrets*, Gothic Image Publications, 1992

—— *Shamanism and the Mystery Lines*: *Ley Lines, Spirit Paths, Shape-shifting and Out-of-body Travel*, Quantum, 1992

—— *The New Ley Hunter's Guide* (combines material from *The Ley Hunter's Companion* 1979 and *The Ley Guide* 1987), Gothic Image Publications, 1994

Dyer, James, *Southern England*: *An Archaeological Guide* (*The Prehistoric and Roman remains*), Faber and Faber, 1973

—— *The Penguin Guide to Prehistoric England and Wales*, Penguin Books, 1981

Ellis, Peter Berresford, *Dictionary of Celtic Mythology*, Constable, 1992

—— *Celtic Dawn*, Constable, 1995

Fidler, J. Havelock, *Ley Lines*: *Their Nature and Properties*: *A Dowser's Investigation*, Turnstone Press, 1983

Fisher, Adrian, & Georg Gerster, *The Art of the Maze*, Weidenfeld and Nicolson, 1990

Gettings, Fred, *Encyclopedia of Secret Knowledge*, Ebury Press, 1995

Gordon, Stuart, *The Encyclopedia of Myths and Legends*, Headline Book Publishing, 1993

Graves, Tom, *Needles of Stone Revisited* (Revised edition of *Needles of Stone*, first published 1978), Gothic Image Publications, 1986

Green, Miranda, *The Gods of the Celts*, Alan Sutton, 1986

—— *Symbol and Image in Celtic Religious Art*, Routledge, 1989

—— *Dictionary of Celtic Myth and Legend*, Thames and Hudson, 1992

Hadingham, Evan, *Ancient Carvings in Britain*: *A Mystery*, Garnstone Press, 1974

—— *Circles and Standing Stones*, William Heinemann, 1975

—— *Early Man and the Cosmos*, William Heinemann, 1983

Heggie, Douglas C., *Megalithic Science: Ancient Mathematics and Astronomy in Northwest Europe*, Thames and Hudson, 1981

Heselton, Philip, *The Elements of Earth Mysteries*, Element, 1991

Hough, Peter, *Supernatural Britain: A Guide to Britain's Most Haunted Locations*, Piatkus Books, 1994

Houlder, Christopher, Wales: An Archeological Guide (The Prehistoric, Roman and Early Medieval Field Monuments), Faber and Faber, 1974

Howard, Michael, *The Runes and Other Magical Alphabets*, Thorsons Publishers, 1978

—— *Earth Mysteries*, Robert Hale, 1990

Hutton, Ronald, *The Pagan Religions of the Ancient British Isles: Their Nature and Legacy*, Blackwell Publishers, 1991

Kightly, Charles, *The Customs and Ceremonies of Britain: An Encyclopaedia of Living Traditions*, Thames and Hudson, 1986

Knight, Gareth, *The Secret Tradition in Arthurian Legend*, Aquarian Press, 1983

Krupp, E.C. (ed.), *In Search of Ancient Astronomies*, Chatto & Windus, 1980; Penguin Books, 1984

Lehan, Brendan, *Early Celtic Christianity*, Constable, 1995

Lonegren, Sig, *Spiritual Dowsing*, Gothic Image Publications, 1986

MacKie, Euan W., *Scotland: An Archaeological Guide: From Earliest Times to the 12th Century AD*, Faber and Faber Ltd, 1975

—— *Science and Society in Prehistoric Britain*, Elek Books, 1977

—— *The Megalith Builders*, Phaidon Press, 1977

McMann, Jean, *Riddles of the Stone Age: Rock Carvings of Ancient Europe*, Thames and Hudson, 1980

Malone, Caroline, *English Heritage Book of Avebury*, B.T. Batsford, 1989

Maltwood, K.E., *A Guide to Glastonbury's Temple of the Stars* (Their giant effigies described from air views, maps, and from 'The High History of the Holy Grail'), James Clarke & Co., first published 1929

Manley, John, *Atlas of Prehistoric Britain*, Phaedon Press, 1989

Meaden, George Terence, *The Goddess of the Stones: The Language of the Megaliths*, Souvenir Press, 1991

—— *The Stonehenge Solution: Sacred Marriage and the Goddess*, Souvenir Press, 1992

Merrifield, Ralph, *The Archaeology of Ritual and Magic*, B.T. Batsford, 1987

Michell, John, *The Old Stones of Land's End*, Garnstone Press, 1974

—— *The Earth Spirit*: *Its Ways, Shrines and Mysteries*, Art and Imagination series, Thames and Hudson, 1975

—— *A Little History of Astro-Archaeology*: *Stages in the Transformation of a Heresy*, Thames and Hudson, 1977; updated and enlarged edition, 1989

—— *Megalithomania*: *Artists, Antiquarians and Archaeologists at the Old Stone Monuments*, Thames and Hudson, 1982

—— *The New View over Atlantis* (fully revised and reset edition of *The View over Atlantis*, first published in 1969) Thames and Hudson, 1983

—— *The Traveller's Key to Sacred England*: *A Guide to the Legends, Lore, and Landscape of England's Sacred Places*, Harrap Columbus, 1989

—— *At the Centre of the World*: *Polar Symbolism Discovered in Celtic, Norse and other Ritualized Landscapes*, Thames and Hudson, 1994

Miller, Hamish & Paul Broadhurst, *The Sun and the Serpent* (An investigation into earth energies by tracking one of the world's most famous ley lines – the St Michael Line), Pendragon Press, 1989

Newman, Paul, *Gods and Graven Images*: *The Chalk Hill-Figures of Britain*, Robert Hale, 1987

Pearson, Michael Parker, *English Heritage Book of Bronze Age Britain*, B.T. Batsford, 1993

Pennick, Nigel, *The Ancient Science of Geomancy*: *Man in Harmony with the Earth*, Thames and Hudson, 1979

—— *Lost Lands and Sunken Cities*, Fortean Tomes, 1987

—— *Earth Harmony*: *Siting and Protecting your Home – A Practical and Spiritual Guide*, Century, 1987

——& Paul Devereux, *Lines on the Landscape*: *Leys and Other Linear Enigmas*, Robert Hale, 1989

—— *Mazes and Labyrinths*, Robert Hale, 1990

Piggott, Stuart, *The Druids*, Thames and Hudson, 1968; Penguin Books, 1974

Rahtz, Philip, *English Heritage Book of Glastonbury*, B.T. Batsford, 1993

Rattue, James, *The Living Stream*: *Holy Wells in Historical Context*, Boydell & Brewer, 1995

Ritchie, Graham and Anna, *Scotland*: *Archaeology and Early History*, Thames and Hudson, 1981

Robins, Don, *Circles of Silence* (Dragon Project), Souvenir Press, 1985

—— *The Secret Language of Stone*: *A New Theory Linking Stones and Crystals with Psychic Phenomena*, Rider, 1988

Ross, Anne, *Pagan Celtic Britain*: *Studies in Iconography and Tradition*, Routledge & Kegan Paul, 1967; Constable, revised edition 1992

—— & Michael Cyprien, *A Traveller's Guide to Celtic Britain*, Routledge & Kegan Paul, 1985

Screeton, Paul, *Quicksilver Heritage: The Mystic Leys – Their Legacy of Ancient Wisdom*, Thorsons Publishers, 1974

Senior, Michael, *Myths of Britain*, Guild Publishing, 1979

Sharples, Niall M., *English Heritage Book of Maiden Castle*, B.T. Batsford, 1991

Shoesmith, Ron, *Alfred Watkins: A Herefordshire Man*, Logaston Press, 1990

Shuel, Brian, *The National Trust Guide to Traditional Customs of Britain*, Webb & Bower/Michael Joseph, 1985

Simpson, Jacqueline, *British Dragons*, B.T. Batsford, 1980

Skinner, Stephen, *The Living Earth Manual of Feng-Shui*, Routledge & Kegan Paul, 1982

Straffon, Cheryl, *Pagan Cornwall – Land of the Goddess*, Meyn Mamvro Publications, 1993

Thom, A., *Megalithic Sites in Britain*, Oxford University Press, 1967

—— *Megalithic Lunar Observatories*, Oxford University Press, 1971

—— & A.S. Thom, *Megalithic Remains in Britain and Brittany*, Oxford University Press, 1978

Thomas, Charles, *Celtic Britain*, Thames and Hudson, 1986

—— *English Heritage Book of Tintagel: Arthur and Archaeology*, B.T. Batsford, 1993

Toulson, Shirley, *The Winter Solstice*, Jill Norman & Hobhouse, 1981

Watkins, Alfred, *The Old Straight Track: Its Mounds, Beacons, Moats, Sites and Mark Stones*, Methuen & Co., 1925; Garnstone Press, 1970

—— *The Ley Hunter's Manual: A Guide to Early Tracks*, The Watkins Meter Co., Hereford, & Simpkin, Marshall & Co., London, 1927; with introduction by John Michell, Turnstone Press, 1983

Weir, Anthony, & James Jerman, *Images of Lust: Sexual Carvings on Medieval Churches*, B.T. Batsford, 1986

Westwood, Jennifer, *Albion: A Guide to Legendary Britain*, Granada Publishing, 1985

Williamson, Tom, & Liz Bellamy, *Ley Lines in Question*, World's Work, 1983

The following is a list of worthwhile magazines on earth mysteries topics that are being published at the time of writing.

3rd Stone (The magazine for the new antiquarian), PO Box 258, Cheltenham, GL53 OHR

The Ley Hunter (The journal of geomancy and earth mysteries), PO Box 92, Penzance, Cornwall, TR18 2XL

Mercian Mysteries (Alternative Studies of Past and Place in the Midlands), 2 Cross Hill Close, Wymeswold, Loughborough. Leics, LE12 6UJ

Meyn Mamvro (Ancient stones and sacred sites in Cornwall), 51 Carn Bosavern, St Just, Penzance, Cornwall, TR19 7QX

Northern Earth (Earth mysteries, antiquarianism and cultural tradition), 10 Jubilee Street, Mytholmroyd, Hebden Bridge, West Yorkshire, HX7 5NP

Source (The holy wells journal), Pen-y-Bont, Bont Newydd, Cefn, St Asaph, Clwyd, LL17 0HH

Wisht Maen (Devon earth mysteries), Condors, Exeter Street, North Tawton, Devon, EX20 2HB

Mail-order booksellers stocking books on earth mysteries and related subjects include:

APRA Books, 443 Meadow Lane, Nottingham, NG2 3GB, Phone 0115 9470372. Fax 0115 9470398.

Awen Books, 10 Jubilee Street, Mytholmroyd, Hebden Bridge, West Yorkshire, HX4 5NP, Phone 01422 882441.

Lionel Beer, 115 Hollybush Lane, Hampton, Middlesex, TW12 2QY, Phone 0181 979 3148.

David & Chris Bland, 20 Belvoir Gardens, Skircoat Green, Halifax, Yorkshire, HX3 0NF, Phone 01422 351212. Fax 01422 345159.

Empress Bookservice, PO Box 92, Penzance, Cornwall, TR18 2XL.

Excalibur Books, Rivenoak, 1 Hillside Gardens, Bangor, Co. Down, BT19 6SJ, Northern Ireland, Phone 01247 458579.

Midnight Books (Frances & Steven Shipp), The Mount, Ascerton Road, Sidmouth, Devon, EX10 9BT, Phone 01395 515446.

T.T. Randall Welton Hill Cottage, West Road, Midsomer Norton, Bath, BA3 2TL, Phone 01761 418926.

Of further interest . . .

DICTIONARY OF SYMBOLIC AND
MYTHOLOGICAL ANIMALS

J. C. Cooper

From ancient times people have ascribed certain powers and significance to the birds and beasts around them, and folk tales, rituals and symbolism have emerged to describe and interpret the creatures of the real and imaginary worlds.

What is the heraldic significance of the dragon? Why is the beaver a sacred animal to the Blackfeet People of North America? How far-reaching is the cult of the werewolf and what are the roots of superstitions about black cats? Drawn from a wealth of cultural sources, this dictionary offers an enlightening account of the role that animals real and fantastical have played in shaping the myths, religions and customs of the world, from primordial times to the present day.

J. C. Cooper was born in China and has travelled extensively throughout the world. She is a lecturer in philosophy and the author of numerous books on Chinese philosophy and world mythology.

DICTIONARY OF SYMBOLS

Tom Chetwynd

Just as we dream every night without necessarily being aware of having dreamed, so our waking life is full of symbolism operating on an unconscious level. Drawn from the collective wisdom of the great psychologists, particularly Jung, this comprehensive and thought-provoking guide explains the language of symbols. Tom Chetwynd describes the major characteristics that recur in all symbolic material; identifying them can enable us to recognize the patterns and processes at work in our own minds, and to explore, develop and transform ourselves.

Tom Chetwynd studied theology at London University and wrote a number of novels and stories before turning his attention to exploring the unconscious with his *Dictionary for Dreamers*, followed by this *Dictionary of Symbols*.

DICTIONARY OF ALCHEMY

Mark Haeffner

Alchemy is a spiritual tradition which has flourished since the beginning of recorded history, if not earlier. Its popular definition – an arcane art of transmuting base metals into gold – is far from the full picture. The true meaning of alchemical concepts lies hidden within a complex structure of archetypal images and symbols.

The Dictionary of Alchemy is the essential reference book to guide you through the labyrinth of pre-Newtonian science and philosophy. It includes both the materialist dimension of the search for the elixir of life and the transmutation of metals, and the inner search for the gold of mystical illumination. This mine of information covers not only the Western Tradition, but also the less well-known, yet equally important, Indo-Tibetan and Chinese Taoist traditions.

DICTIONARY OF MIND, BODY AND SPIRIT

IDEAS, PEOPLE AND PLACES

Eileen Campbell and J. H. Brennan

In our fast-changing world, many people are uneasy with the values that have grown out of a scientific, reductionist world view and are exploring different ideas and approaches. People are looking for answers to life's seemingly unanswerable questions. This dictionary will prove a useful starting-point. It covers a whole range of subjects – spiritual and esoteric traditions, paranormal phenomenal, people and places – from acupressure to automatic writing, Spiritualism to Santeria, Zen to Zoroastrianism.

DICTIONARY OF SYMBOLIC & MYTHOLOGICAL ANIMALS	0 7225 3238 5	£7.99	☐
DICTIONARY OF SYMBOLS	1 85538 296 2	£8.99	☐
DICTIONARY OF ALCHEMY	0 85538 440 X	£6.99	☐
DICTIONARY OF MIND, BODY AND SPIRIT	1 85538 328 4	£6.99	☐

All these books are available from your local bookseller or can be ordered direct from the publishers.

To order direct just tick the titles you want and fill in the form below:

Name: _____

Address: _____

_____

_____ Postcode: _____

Send to: Thorsons Mail Order, Dept 3, HarperCollins*Publishers*, Westerhill Road, Bishopbriggs, Glasgow G64 2QT.
Please enclose a cheque or postal order or your authority to debit your Visa/Access account —

Credit card no: _____

Expiry date: _____

Signature: _____

— to the value of the cover price plus:
UK & BFPO: Add £1.00 for the first book and 25p for each additional book ordered.
Overseas orders including Eire: Please add £2.95 service charge. Books will be sent by surface mail but quotes for airmail despatches will be given on request.

24 HOUR TELEPHONE ORDERING SERVICE FOR ACCESS/VISA CARDHOLDERS – TEL: 0141 772 2281.